Mindfulness at Work Essentials

FOR DUMMIES®

A Wiley Brand

by Shamash Alidina
Juliet Adams

FOR DUMMIES®

A Wiley Brand

Mindfulness at Work Essentials For Dummies®

Published by
Wiley Publishing Australia Pty Ltd
42 McDougall Street
Milton, Qld 4064
www.dummies.com

Copyright © 2015 Wiley Publishing Australia Pty Ltd

Authorised adaptation of *Mindfulness at Work For Dummies, Portable Edition*
© 2014 John Wiley & Sons, Ltd. (9781118965856).

The moral rights of the authors have been asserted.

National Library of Australia
Cataloguing-in-Publication data:

Author:	Alidina, Shamash
Title:	Mindfulness at Work Essentials For Dummies / Shamash Alidina, Juliet Adams.
ISBN:	9780730319498 (pbk.)
	9780730319481 (ebook)
Series:	For Dummies.
Notes:	Includes index.
Subjects:	Psychology — industrial.
	Employees — coaching of.
	Success in business — psychological aspects.
Other authors/ Contributors:	Adams, Juliet, author.
Dewey Number:	158.7

All rights reserved. No part of this book, including interior design, cover design and icons, may be reproduced or transmitted in any form, by any means (electronic, photocopying, recording or otherwise) without the prior written permission of the Publisher. Requests to the Publisher for permission should be addressed to the Legal Services section of John Wiley & Sons Australia, Ltd, Level 2, 155 Cremorne Street, Richmond, Vic 3151, or email auspermissions@wiley.com.

Cover image: © iStock.com/filmfoto

Typeset by diacriTech, Chennai, India

Printed in Singapore by
C.O.S. Printers Pte Ltd

10 9 8 7 6 5 4 3 2 1

Contents at a Glance

Table of Contents

Introduction

*M*indfulness is a mental discipline and way of being that has been practised for thousands of years. Modern science has researched mindfulness as a secular practice and discovered its tremendous power-creating positive changes in the brain that have never been seen before in brain scans.

Mindfulness was initially used in medical settings in the late 1970s. In the decades that followed, the use of mindfulness throughout western society began to rapidly increase. Nowadays, many organisations offer staff mindfulness training to help their employees boost their resilience, productivity, emotional intelligence, focus, or even just to help them feel happier!

Mindfulness at Work Essentials For Dummies offers an accessible and comprehensive look at different ways to bring greater mindfulness into the workplace setting, whatever your motivation.

This book is for anyone with any sort of role in the workplace. Employees, small-business owners, managers and corporate executives will find practical application from this book, we hope. We even explore mindful leadership.

We wrote this book because we're passionate about mindfulness! Having practised mindfulness both in our personal and professional lives, we can see the massive positive benefits that practising mindfulness can offer, such as greater creativity, improved communication and higher levels of productivity and wellbeing.

We also feel mindfulness can help individuals better manage the negative consequences of the demanding modern workplace environment. High levels of pressure, tight deadlines and overly demanding managers can take their toll on the toughest individuals. With stress now one of the leading causes of absence from work according to the World Health Organization, the need to find ways of building mental resilience is huge. We like to think that mindfulness offers a powerful way of raising resilience in the workplace setting, and workplace-specific mindfulness research is starting to support this.

With many organisations, big and small, now offering mindfulness at work, this book offers many practical ways to integrate mindfulness in the workplace. We aim to simplify the concepts without losing their subtle essence, and include lots of exercises for everyone to try out, from the boardroom to the shop floor. We hope *Mindfulness at Work Essentials For Dummies* will have something for you and offers you a fresh approach to your work.

About This Book

Mindfulness at Work Essentials For Dummies provides you with practical techniques to integrate mindfulness into the workplace. Each chapter is jam-packed with insights about the art of mindfulness, how to be mindful quickly and easily, and how to work with mindful awareness. This book has been written for beginners to the idea of mindfulness and those looking for ways to introduce mindfulness into their organisation in a scientifically proven way.

Within this book, you may note that some web addresses break across two lines of text. If you're reading this book in print and want to visit one of these web pages, simply key in the web address exactly as it's noted in the text, pretending as though the line break doesn't exist. If you're reading this as an ebook, you've got it easy — just click the address to be taken directly to the page online.

Foolish Assumptions

In writing this book, we made a few assumptions about who you are:

- ✔ You work on a regular basis, or are actively seeking work.
- ✔ You're looking for an approach to improve your and your staff's success in the workplace.
- ✔ You want to be more mindful at work, but don't know where to start.

✔ You are willing to try the various mindfulness exercises and strategies we have suggested several times before judging if they could work for you or your staff.

✔ You're looking for long-term ways of improving your effectiveness in the workplace rather than just a quick fix.

Beyond these, we've not assumed too much, we hope. This book is for you whether you're male or female, aged 18 upwards.

Icons Used in This Book

Scattered through the book you'll see various icons to guide you on your way. Icons are a *For Dummies* way of drawing your attention to important stuff, interesting stuff and stuff you really need to know not to do.

This is stuff you need to know: Whatever else you carry away from this book, note these bits with care.

Handy tidbits to help you get nice and mindful at work.

An activity for you to try out for yourself, including some free online tools available at www.dummies.com/go/mawessentials.

Where to Go from Here

We've compiled this book so that you can dip in and out as you please. We invite you to make good use of the Table of Contents (or the index) and jump straight into the section you fancy. You're in charge and it's up to you.

We wish you all the best in your quest to be mindful or to bring mindfulness to others at work, and hope you find something of use within these pages.

Five Ways to Be More Mindful at Work

- **Be consciously present.** Mindfulness is about being aware and awake rather than operating unconsciously. When you're consciously present at work, you're aware of what's going on around you and what's going on within you.

- **Use short exercises at work.** Mindful exercises train your brain to be more mindful. The more exercises you do, the more easily your brain can drop into a mindful state, optimising your brain function.

- **Slow down to speed up.** Being in a panicky rush leads to bad decisions and is a misuse of energy. Instead, pause, focus on listening, stroll rather than run, and generally take your time when you're at work.

- **Make stress your friend.** The next time you're facing a challenge at work, notice how your heart rate speeds up and your breathing accelerates. Observe these responses and then switch your attitude — respond to your stress creatively rather than negatively. Be grateful that the stress response is energising you.

- **Use mindful reminders.** Set an alarm, put mindfulness in your calendar, write a small note or picture and keep it on your desk. All these things will help you come back into the present moment, to see yourself and your surroundings afresh. They help you take a small step back and reflect rather than react to what's coming at you in the form of demands, tasks and challenges.

Visit dummies.com for free access to great *For Dummies* content online.

Chapter 1

Exploring Mindfulness in the Workplace

*I*n tough economic times, many organisations are looking for new ways to deliver better products and services to customers while simultaneously reducing costs. Carrying on as normal isn't an option. Organisations are looking for sustainable ways to be more innovative. Leaders must really engage staff, and everyone needs to become more resilient in the face of ongoing change. For these reasons, more and more organisations are offering staff training in mindfulness.

This chapter talks about what mindfulness is and why so many leading organisations are investing in it.

Becoming More Mindful at Work

In this section you discover what mindfulness is. More importantly, you also discover what mindfulness is not! You also find out why mindfulness has become so important in the modern-day workplace.

Clarifying what mindfulness is

Have you ever driven somewhere and arrived at your destination remembering nothing about your journey? Or grabbed a snack and noticed a few moments later that all you have left is an empty packet? Most people have! These are common examples of 'mindlessness', or 'going on auto-pilot'.

Like many humans, you're probably 'not present' for much of your own life. You may fail to notice the good things in your life or hear what your body is telling you. You probably also make your life harder than it needs to be by poisoning yourself with toxic self-criticism.

Mindfulness can help you to become more aware of your thoughts, feelings and sensations in a way that suspends judgement and self-criticism. Developing the ability to pay attention to and see clearly whatever is happening moment by moment does not eliminate life's pressures, but it can help you respond to them in a more productive, calmer manner.

Learning and practising mindfulness can help you to recognise and step away from habitual, often unconscious emotional and physiological reactions to everyday events. Practising mindfulness allows you to be fully present in your life and work and improves your quality of life.

Mindfulness can help you to recognise, slow down or stop automatic and habitual reactions, and see situations with greater focus and clarity.

Mindfulness at work is all about developing awareness of thoughts, emotions and physiology and how they interact with one another. Mindfulness is also about being aware of your surroundings, helping you better understand the needs of those around you.

Mindfulness training is like going to the gym. In the same way as training a muscle, you can train your brain to direct your attention to where you want it to be. In simple terms, mindfulness is all about managing your mind.

Recognising what mindfulness isn't

Misleading myths about mindfulness abound. Here are a few:

Myth 1: 'I will need to visit a Buddhist centre, go on a retreat or travel to the Far East to learn mindfulness.'

Experienced mindfulness instructors are operating all over the world. Many teachers now teach mindfulness to groups of staff in the workplace. One-to-one mindfulness teaching can be delivered in the office, in hotel meeting rooms or even via the web. Some people do attend retreats after learning mindfulness if they want to deepen their knowledge, experience peace and quiet, or gain further tuition, but doing so isn't essential.

Myth 2: 'Practising mindfulness will conflict with my religious beliefs.'

Mindfulness isn't a religion. For example, Mindfulness-Based Stress Reduction (MBSR) and Mindfulness-Based Cognitive Therapy (MBCT) are entirely secular — as are most workplace programmes. No religious belief of any kind is necessary. Mindfulness can help you step back from your mental noise and tune in to your own innate wisdom. Mindfulness is practised by people of all faiths and by those with no spiritual beliefs.

Myth 3: 'I'm too busy to sit and be quiet for any length of time.'

When you're busy, the thought of sitting and 'doing nothing' may seem like the last thing you want to do. Just 15 minutes a day spent practising mindfulness can help you to become more productive and less distracted. Then you'll be able to make the most of your busy day and get more done in less time. When you first start practising mindfulness, you'll almost certainly experience mental distractions, but if you persevere you'll find it easier to tune out distractions and to manage your mind. As time goes on, your ability to concentrate increases as does your sense of wellbeing and feeling of control over your life.

Myth 4: 'Mindfulness and meditation are one and the same. Mindfulness is just a trendy new name.'

Fact: Mindfulness often involves specific meditation practices. **Fiction:** All meditation is the same.

Many popular forms of meditation are all about relaxation — leaving your troubles behind and imagining yourself in a calm and tranquil 'special place' Mindfulness helps you to find out how to live with your life in the present moment rather than run away from it. Mindfulness is about approaching life and things that you find difficult and exploring them with openness, rather than avoiding them. Most people find that practising mindfulness does help them to relax, but that this relaxation is a welcome by-product, not the objective.

Training your attention: The power of focus

Are you one of the millions of workers who routinely put in long hours, often for little or no extra pay? In the current climate of cutbacks, job losses and 'business efficiencies', many people feel the need to work longer hours just to keep on top of their workload. However, research shows that working longer hours does not mean that you get more done. Actually, if you continue to work when past your peak, your performance slackens off and continues to do so as time goes on (see Chapter 4).

Discovering how to focus and concentrate better is the key to maintaining peak performance. Recognising when you've slipped past peak performance and then taking steps to bring yourself back to peak is also vital. Mindfulness comes in at this point. Over time, it helps you focus your attention to where you want it to be.

Applying mindful attitudes

Practising mindfulness involves more than just training your brain to focus. It also teaches you some alternative mindful attitudes to life's challenges. You discover the links between your thoughts, emotions and physiology. You find out that what's important isn't what happens to you, but how you choose to respond. This statement may sound simple, but most people respond to situations based on their mental programming (past experiences and predictions of what will happen next). Practising mindfulness makes you more aware of how your thoughts, emotions and physiology impact on your responses to people and situations. This awareness then enables you to choose how to respond rather than reacting on auto-pilot. You may well find that you respond in a different manner.

By gaining a better understanding of your brain's response to life events, you can use mindfulness techniques to reduce your *fight-or-flight* response and regain your body's 'rest and relaxation' state. You will see things more clearly and get more done.

Mindfulness also brings you face to face with your inner bully — the voice in your head that says you're not talented enough, not smart enough or not good enough. By learning to treat thoughts like these as 'just mental processes and not facts', the inner bully loses its grip on your life and you become free to reach your full potential.

These examples are just a few of the many ways that a mindful attitude can have a positive impact on your life and career prospects.

Finding Out Why Your Brain Needs Mindfulness

Recent advances in brain-scanning technology are helping us to understand why our brain needs mindfulness. In this section you discover powerful things about your brain — its evolution, its hidden rules, how thoughts shape your brain structure, and the basics of how your brain operates at work.

Discovering your brain's hidden rules

Imagine yourself as one of your ancient ancestors — a cave dweller. In ancient times you had to make life-or-death decisions every day. You had to decide whether it was best to approach a reward (such as killing a deer for food) or avoid a threat (such as a fierce predator charging at you). If you failed to gain your reward, in this example a deer to eat, you'd probably live to hunt another day. But, if you failed to avoid the threat, you'd be dead, never to hunt again.

As a result of facing these daily dangers, your brain has evolved to minimise threat. Unfortunately, this has led to the brain spending much more time looking for potential risks and problems than seeking rewards and embracing new opportunities. This tendency is called 'the human negativity bias'.

When your brain detects a potential threat, it floods your system with powerful hormones designed to help you evade mortal danger. The sudden flood of dozens of hormones into your body results in your heart rate speeding up, blood pressure increasing, pupils dilating and veins constricting to send more blood to major muscle groups to help you sprint away from danger. More oxygen is pumped into your lungs, and non-essential systems (such as digestion, the immune system, and routine body repair and maintenance) shut down to provide more energy for emergency functions. Your brain starts to have trouble focusing on small tasks because it's trying to maintain focus on the big picture to anticipate and avoid further threat.

Threat or risk avoidance is controlled by the primitive areas of your brain, which operate quickly. This speed explains why, when you unexpectedly encounter a snake in the woods, your *primitive brain* decides on the best way to keep you safe from harm with no conscious thought and you jump out of the way long before your *higher brain* engages to find a rational solution.

This process is great from an evolutionary perspective, but can be bad news in modern-day life. Many people routinely overestimate the potential threat involved in everyday work such as a critical boss, a failed presentation or social humiliation. These modern-day 'threats' are treated by the brain in exactly the same way as your ancestor's response to mortal danger. This fight-or-flight response was designed to be used for short periods of time. Unfortunately, when under pressure at work it can remain activated for long periods of time. This activation can lead to poor concentration, inability to focus, low immunity and even serious illness.

Mindfulness training helps you to recognise when you're in this heightened state of arousal and be able to reduce or even switch off the fight-or-flight response. It also helps you develop the skill to trigger at will your 'rest and relaxation' response, bringing your body back to normal, allowing it to repair itself, and increasing both your sense of wellbeing and ability to focus on work.

Recognising that you are what you think

For many years it was thought that once you reached a certain age your brain became fixed. We now know that the adult brain retains impressive powers of *neuroplasticity*; that is, the ability to change its structure and function in response to experience. It was also believed that, if you damaged certain areas of the brain (as a result of a stroke or other brain injury), you'd no longer be capable of performing certain brain functions. We now know that in some cases the brain can re-wire itself and train a different area to undertake the functions that the damaged part previously carried out. The brain's hard wiring (neural pathways) change constantly in response to thoughts and experiences.

Neuroplasticity offers amazing opportunities to reinvent yourself and change the way you do and think about things. Your unique brain wiring is a result of your thoughts and experiences in life.

Blaming your genes or upbringing; saying 'it's not my fault, that's how I was born' is no longer a good excuse!

In order to take advantage of this knowledge, you need to develop awareness of your thoughts, and the impact that these thoughts have on your emotions and physiology. The problem is that, if you're like most people, you're probably rarely aware of the majority of your thoughts. Let's face it; you'd be exhausted if you were. Mindfulness helps you to develop the ability to passively observe your thoughts as mental processes. In turn, this allows you to observe patterns of thought and decide whether these patterns are appropriate and serve you well. If you decide that they don't, your awareness of them gives you the opportunity to replace them with better ways of thinking and behaving.

Another common problem you may encounter is that, although you may *think* that your decisions and actions are always based on present-moment facts, in reality they rarely are. Making decisions based on your brain's prediction of the future (which is usually based on your past experiences and unique brain wiring) is common. In addition, you see with your brain; in other words, your brain acts as a filter to incoming information from the eyes and picks out what it thinks is important. The problem with all of this is that you routinely make decisions and act without full possession of the facts. What happened in the past will not necessarily happen now; your predictions about the future could be inaccurate, leading to inappropriate responses and actions.

Practising mindfulness helps you to see the bigger picture and make decisions based on present-moment facts rather than self-generated assumptions and fiction.

Mindfulness helps you to notice when your thoughts begin to spiral and to take action to stop them spiralling downwards even further. You can observe what's going on in the present moment, and separate present-moment facts from self-created fiction. This ability gives you choices and a world of new possibilities.

Think of a person or situation that triggers your primitive brain's threat system. (Don't pick anything too scary or threatening!)

1. **Observe what's going on in your head.** Identify patterns of thoughts, as if you were a spectator observing from the outside. What is it specifically that has triggered your primitive brain?

2. **Acknowledge your emotional response without judgement or self-blame.** Try to observe from a distance and see if you can reduce or prevent a strong emotional reaction by observing the interplay of your thoughts and emotions as if you were a bystander.

3. **Be kind to yourself.** You're human, and just responding according to your mental wiring. Observe both your thoughts and emotions as simply 'mental processes', without the need to respond to them. Regarding them as 'thoughts not facts' and being kind to yourself helps to encourage your primitive brain to let go of the steering wheel and allow your higher brain to become the driver once more.

When developing new neural pathways, practice makes perfect. Changing your behaviour or learning to do something new takes awareness, intention, action and practice — no short cuts exist! Understanding a few simple facts about how your brain works and making small adjustments to your responses can help you to create new, more productive, neural pathways.

Exploring your brain at work

Before diving into more detail about mindfulness, and how it can be of benefit to your work, you need to discover a little more about how your brain processes everyday work tasks.

Mindfulness shows you how to mentally stand back and observe what's going on around you and in your brain. It also helps you to develop different approaches to life that are kinder to you and usually more productive. Mindfulness helps you observe and reduce the mental chatter that distracts you from your work, allowing you to focus on it more fully. By intentionally taking steps to recognise and avoid distractions and focusing your full attention on one task at a time, you can get things done more quickly, with fewer mistakes and less repetition. Using mindfulness techniques when you feel your attention waning can help you to restart work feeling refreshed and focused.

Mindfulness can also be useful in high-level meetings when emotions can sometimes be charged. In *avoidance mode*, people are motivated by the desire to avoid something happening. With their threat system activated, they may fail to see the bigger picture, be less able to think clearly, and be less creative in their ideas and solutions. Often the effort taken to avoid something happening is disproportionate to dealing with the thing you seek to avoid. On the other hand, in *approach mode* you're able to explore new possibilities and opportunities with an open mind.

When working in avoidance mode, cognitive thinking resources are diminished, making it harder to think and work things through. You're also likely to feel less positive and engaged.

The brain can have a significant impact on how you work. Finding out about and practising mindfulness gives you the tools you need to harness this knowledge to manage your mind better.

Starting Your Mindful Journey

Congratulations! The fact that you've picked up this book and started reading it means that you've already started your mindful journey. The chapters in this book describe lots of ways to learn mindfulness, one of which is sure to suit your learning style and fit in with your busy life. You'll also discover that mindfulness involves much more than sitting down and focusing on your breath. In this book, you should find a number of mindfulness techniques that work for you.

A good book is a great starting point, but nothing can replace experiencing mindfulness for yourself. As with learning anything new, you may find it difficult to know where to start. Learning mindfulness from an experienced teacher who can help you to overcome obstacles and guide your development is advisable. The idea behind this book is to demonstrate *how* and *why* mindfulness can benefit you at work, and provide suggestions of how to apply simple mindfulness techniques to everyday work challenges.

Being mindful at work yourself

Getting caught up in the manic pace of everyday work life is common. You, like many workers, may feel under pressure to deliver more with fewer resources. You may also be keen to demonstrate what an asset you are to your company by working longer and longer hours, and being contactable round the clock.

Being mindful at work can involve as little or as much change as you're able to accommodate at this moment in time. At one end of the scale, you may simply apply knowledge of how the brain works and some mindful principles to your work. To gain maximum benefit, you need to practise mindfulness regularly and apply quick mindfulness techniques in the workplace when you need to regain focus or encounter difficulties. The choice is yours! The benefits you gain increase in line with the effort you put in. You should see a real difference after practising mindfulness for as little as ten minutes a day for about six weeks.

Following these initial practice sessions, most people then introduce a few short mindfulness techniques at work. Over time, as mindfulness becomes second nature to you, you'll develop the ability to practise wherever and whenever the opportunity arises. As your confidence builds and you apply mindfulness to your work further, others will probably notice changes in you. You may appear calmer, more poised and better focused. Possibly your work relationships have improved. If you're lucky enough to be offered mindfulness sessions in work time, don't be surprised if people are curious, and ask you for tips and techniques to try out for themselves. Organisations that offer mindfulness classes often have a long waiting list of staff eager to attend.

Overcoming common challenges

Probably the most common challenges you face when learning mindfulness are finding the right time and place to practise, and breaking down habits and mindsets in order to do things differently.

You now need to address each of these challenges in turn.

Finding the right time and place to practise

If you're lucky enough to be offered mindfulness training by your organisation, you will quickly discover that mindfulness is unlike any other course you've attended. Unlike most courses that employers routinely offer to staff, simply attending isn't enough. Classes help you understand the principles that underpin mindfulness and how mindfulness techniques work. They also provide you with a safe environment and guidance to try out different mindfulness techniques. However, the real learning usually happens outside work, as you practise it. You can't get fit without exercising, can you? The same applies to mindfulness. Think of mindfulness as a good workout for your brain; the more you practise, the easier it becomes.

On a typical workplace mindfulness course, you're taught a different technique each week, which you need to practise for at least six days before moving on to the next one. This process can prove to be one of the most challenging aspects of learning mindfulness. For many busy workers, their entire day is scheduled, and sometimes extends into their home life. With a mindset of 'so much to do and so little time', even finding 10–15 minutes a day can feel daunting. The question to ask yourself is, 'Why am I doing this?' For many people, the answer is, 'Because I can't continue working in the way I do.' If this is your reply, re-arranging your life to make time for mindfulness is certainly worthwhile. Try not to think about mindfulness as just another thing that needs to be fitted into your busy life. Rather, view it as a new way to live your life. Think of the time you spend practising mindfulness as 'me time' — after all, this time is one of the rare moments in which you have nothing to do but focus on yourself.

Breaking down habits and mindsets

Habits are formed when you repeat the same thoughts or behaviours many times. Habits are highly efficient from a brain perspective because they're stored in the primitive brain, which can repeat them quickly without any conscious thought, using very little energy.

Learning mindfulness may take effort, especially if you start to challenge your habits and patterns of thinking. Make sure you remember that, just as it takes time to form habits, so it takes time to replace old habits with different ways of thinking and being. With a little time and perseverance you can find new ways of working that are more productive and better for your health and sense of wellbeing.

Creating a mindful workplace

Every great journey starts with just one step. A young, single mother of three was once given the opportunity to climb Mount Everest. Three-quarters of the way up the mountain she became exhausted, felt overwhelmed by the whole journey and declared that she could go no further. The trek leader calmly stood in front of her and asked whether she could see his footsteps in the snow ahead. She nodded in agreement. He told her that all she needed to do was put one foot in front of another, following his footsteps. By focusing on the present-moment action of her feet, she was able to avoid worrying about the remainder of the journey. She made it to the summit — one of the greatest achievements of her life.

Getting caught up in planning the journey ahead is common and at times you may feel overwhelmed by all the things you need to do and think about. When finding out about and practising mindfulness for the first time, focusing only on the next footstep, rather than the journey as a whole, is often the best approach. Try to let your mindful journey unfold, day by day, moment by moment. If you truly want your organisation to become more mindful, you need to start by focusing on yourself. As you gain a deeper understanding of what mindfulness is, and start to experiment with integrating mindfulness into your life and work, you discover for yourself what works and what doesn't. Only then are you equipped to make a real difference to your organisation. The building blocks of a mindful organisation are mindful employees who start to transform their organisations one step at a time. See Chapter 10 for more on mindful organisations.

Living the dream: Mindfulness at work

Sometimes the hardest part of a journey is taking the first step. In this book, you can find a wealth of information about mindfulness. You also discover mindful techniques for different situations that you may encounter at work and for different occupations (see Chapter 6).

The potential of mindfulness to transform the way you work and live your life is immense. The extent to which you benefit from it is entirely up to you and the effort that you're able to put into it.

When discovering how to become more mindful, remember ABC:

- ✔ **A is for awareness.** Becoming more aware of what you're thinking and doing and what's going on in your mind and body.

- ✔ **B is for 'just being' with your experiences.** Avoiding the tendency to respond on auto-pilot and feed problems by creating your own story.

- ✔ **C is for choice.** By seeing things as they are you can *choose* to respond more wisely and by creating a gap between an experience and your reaction, you can step out of auto-pilot, which opens up a world of new possibilities.

As with all new skills, the more you practise mindfulness, the easier it becomes. Canadian psychologist Donald Hebb coined the phrase 'neurones that fire together, wire together'. In other words, the more you practise mindfulness, the more you develop the neural pathways in the brain associated with being mindful.

Chapter 2

Exploring the Benefits of Mindfulness in the Workplace

*M*indfulness may appear to be the 'in thing' at the moment, but does it have any substance? What are the actual benefits of mindfulness at work?

In this chapter we uncover the positive effects of mindfulness for yourself. We discuss the impact of the many positive changes that take place in your own brain as a result of mindfulness practice. We also tell you why so many organisations are training their leaders and employees in mindfulness, and explore organisational ways of integrating mindfulness into the workplace to increase staff performance and wellbeing.

Discovering the Benefits for Employees

Being a mindful employee has many benefits. In this section find out how mindfulness changes your brain and how those changes make you more resilient, emotionally intelligent and focused. If you're in a leadership position, discover how mindfulness can make you more effective in your work too.

Increased mental resilience

Resilience is the process of adapting well when you experience adversity, trauma or a major source of stress. Resilience is sometimes described as the ability to 'bounce back' from difficult experiences.

In the average workplace, mental resilience is essential. If you're resilient, you're able to deal with rapid changes and serious challenges rather than spiralling downwards when faced with difficulties.

Resilience isn't a trait. You're not born with a certain amount of resilience and stuck with it. Instead, resilience involves a combination of thoughts, behaviours and actions that you can learn. That's what makes resilience such an exciting concept.

Let's imagine you've been working on securing a bid for a huge project. You've been developing the presentation and report for months. You're under tremendous pressure to succeed and, when the day comes, your nerves get the better of you. You struggle to answer questions, as your mind goes blank. You imagine losing the contract and your manager shouting at you in frustration and firing you.

If you did fail to secure the contract, the following thoughts might arise: 'I failed. What if I get fired? How will I pay my bills? I should have practised more. I'm pathetic.'

These thoughts emerge from the soup of emotions that's ignited by the stress you've experienced. If you're unmindful, these thoughts persist and you're less able to bounce back from the experience. You feel increasingly worse and things can spiral downwards.

If you practise mindfulness, you notice that you're having these judgemental thoughts. You're then able to step back from them and see that, perhaps the presentation didn't go well, but all the other things you're telling yourself are just thoughts arising from your negative feelings about the event — they aren't necessarily true. By acknowledging that your feelings impact on your thoughts, you can avoid reacting to imagined threats and deal with the situation in a more reasoned manner. Over time, practising mindfulness builds up your resilience to such workplace experiences and you become better able to deal with them.

Even the US Army is using mindfulness to help build resilience in its recruits. Initial studies show that mindfulness helps to develop soldiers' mental fitness so that they're more able to make good decisions in stressful situations and less likely to suffer post-traumatic stress disorder.

Some people mistakenly think that resilient people don't experience distress — that's not true. When adversity strikes, to have mental and emotional pain is normal. Developing resilience, however, ensures that, over time, you're able to rebuild your life.

But, you may be wondering, how does mindfulness increase resilience in your brain? Research by Professor Richard Davidson and colleagues has discovered how mindfulness may help build resilience. They looked at people's brains when faced with a stressor and found that their amygdala (the part of the brain responsible for processing emotions and responding to fear) became activated, releasing stress hormones. The research participants also experienced negative, cyclical thoughts long after the stressor had passed. In those participants who practised mindfulness, however, the activity of the amygdala reduced soon after the stressor was removed. Davidson states that better control of the amygdala may be the *key* to resilience.

Psychologist Barbara Fredrickson believes that mindfulness offers other ways to build resilience too. They are:

- ✓ **Acceptance:** You have the capacity to see what you can change and what you can't.

- ✓ **Self-compassion:** Allows you to be kind to yourself in the face of adversity. You see your difficulties as part and parcel of humanity's struggle with life's challenges. There are over 200 studies showing the positive benefits of self-compassion alone.

- ✓ **Growth:** You're open to seeing difficulties as opportunities to learn and grow. Your mindset is open rather than fixed.

- ✓ **Creativity:** In a more mindful state, the part of your brain geared towards creative thinking is active.

So, following an unsuccessful outcome to months of hard work, you may say to yourself: 'Beating myself up is pointless. I worked hard but I wasn't successful this time. I'm sure there are things I can discover from this experience. Perhaps I could ask for feedback and tips from others and, after a few days

of well-deserved rest, I can have a go at a different project.'
Mindfulness offers a whole different way of being with your
everyday experiences.

Here are five steps you can take to use mindfulness to help build
your resilience:

- ✔ **Help others.** Be mindful of the needs of others rather than
  just yourself. By seeking ways to help others when you're
  not so busy, you're more likely to be supported when going
  through difficulties yourself.

- ✔ **Look after yourself.** In addition to helping others, help
  yourself too! Be mindful of how much sleep you're getting,
  how much exercise you're doing and if you're taking regular
  breaks. Muscles strengthen only if they have time to rest
  between activities. Your brain is the same.

- ✔ **Nudge your mindset.** In any given moment, your brain
  receives far more information than it can actively be
  conscious of. So, rather than focusing the spotlight of your
  attention on what's not going well, focus it on the positives.
  What went well today? What are you grateful for? Your
  brain will thank you for it.

- ✔ **Expect change.** If you practise mindfulness, you know that
  change is the only constant. If you can see that the nature
  of the world is change, and you seek to adapt to the change
  rather than avoid or run away from it, you're being more
  mindful and more resilient.

- ✔ **Seek meaning.** When adversity strikes, as it inevitably
  does, after the initial period of sadness or anger, you do
  have a choice. You can sink into feeling sorry for yourself
  or look for an opportunity for growth. Look out for what
  you can find out from the challenges you're currently
  facing. Be mindful of the opportunities that arise for you.

Improved relationships

You've probably had to work with someone difficult to get on
with. Maybe they're rude, critical and rarely offer praise. They
say the wrong thing at the wrong time. You wonder how they
managed to get into the company in the first place. You may
even think that you're better off avoiding certain colleagues
altogether.

Relationships matter. A lot. In fact, the human brain is designed to be social. Learning, emotional processing, creativity and insight are often enhanced when in conversation with others. If that's the case, why are workplace relationships so often fraught with difficulty? And how does mindfulness improve workplace relationships?

When you're mindful, you're better able to regulate your emotions. For example, Frank works for a large oil company and is responsible for the refining division. He talks to Samantha about her recent lateness at work. She starts giving excuses. This pattern repeats over several days. Eventually, in a fit of anger, Frank starts shouting at her. She shouts back. In the weeks that follow, Samantha comes into work early but her working relationship with Frank deteriorates further.

If Frank were more mindful, he'd have noticed the anger building up inside him. As a result, he could have acknowledged his feelings, and made a conscious choice about what to do next. Speaking to Samantha later in the day when he was more composed might have revealed a bigger underlying issue. Seen in this bigger context, Frank is less likely to react with anger next time, and more likely to develop positive working relationships with colleagues.

Mindfulness improves relationships by enhancing the ability to listen both to the words being said and the emotions behind them. Good communication is at the very heart of relationships. With greater levels of mindful awareness, you become more adept at listening to both the words being spoken and their emotional signals. By giving a person your full attention, the relationship is enhanced.

When engaged in mindfulness, you're also a better listener. You're better able to listen because mindfulness enhances focus. Research shows that the more you practise mindful exercises, the better your brain becomes at focusing on whatever it chooses to. Being better able to focus has obvious benefits when you're trying to listen to someone at work.

Mindfulness also helps you to help others, by seeing the bigger picture. Rather than just thinking about yourself and what you need, you think about others more.

Use the following tips to be more mindful in your workplace relationships:

- ✔ **Really connect.** Make a conscious effort to look people in the eye when they're speaking to you. Listen to their words and try to pick up on their emotions too. If you have the tendency to interrupt, resist it. Listen more and ask questions to clarify what the other person is saying.

- ✔ **Take a mindful pause.** Stop and think before speaking to someone you find difficult. Notice whether you react emotionally to that person and, if you do, try to step back from your habitual emotions and thoughts. If you carry on doing what you've always done, you carry on getting what you've always got. Use the mindful pause and see what effect it has on the relationship.

- ✔ **See things from their viewpoint.** Use mindful awareness to step back and see things from the other person's point of view. Maybe they don't have the necessary social skills, or make rash decisions because they're anxious. Seen in this way, their behaviour may feel less threatening and you may feel sorry for them, not annoyed.

- ✔ **Wish them well.** As you walk about in your workplace, rather than negatively judging people, or even being neutral towards them, you can wish them well. As you encounter people, think to yourself, 'May you be well, may you be happy'. After all, they're human beings just like you, and want to be happy, just like you. By wishing others well, you shift your attention away from your own worries and towards a more positive and mindful mindset.

Honed mental clarity and focus

Imagine lying in a darkened room and shining a torch around. What you can see is whatever that spotlight is shining on.

Your mind works in the same way. Your attention is like a spotlight, and in a moment of mindfulness you can decide where to shine it. You can focus within yourself, on a particular part of your body or even your body as a whole. You can focus on your thoughts or emotions.

Focus is one of the most overlooked skills that humans possess. Most people think that focus is something they do or don't have. But that's not true. Your attention is like a muscle — the more you flex that brain muscle, the stronger it gets. With time and effort, the regions of your brain responsible for maintaining focus will grow. And these changes happen within days, not years. Mindfulness offers a way to train that muscle in your brain so you can decide where you want to focus, and stay focused for longer periods of time.

When you lack focus, you feel scattered. Your attention can get caught by another person's conversation, a thought about the event you attended yesterday or just noise outside. The more your attention snags on other things, the less able you are to complete the tasks in front of you and you begin to feel inefficient. When you practise mindful exercises, your mind gradually shifts from being frazzled to being focused. You then become more efficient and, as a result, have more time to rest and relax.

One of the other benefits of greater focus is greater levels of happiness. Research suggests that people are happiest when they're fully focused on something. That focus can be on anything: Skiing downhill, painting a picture or writing a sales report. When fully focused, people enter a 'flow' state of mind, which results in a heightened feeling of wellbeing. As you develop your ability to focus, you'll enter this flow state more often when working. And if you're happier, you're immediately more creative, productive and confident.

How can you improve your focus in the workplace using mindfulness? Try these tips:

- ✔ **Start the working day with a short mindful exercise.** Try mindfulness of breath or the body scan (for more on these, see Chapter 3). Even a mindful jog in the morning can help.

- ✔ **Avoid multi-tasking as much as possible.** If you can, do one task at a time and give it your full attention. Too much multi-tasking reduces your brain's ability to focus.

- ✔ **Feel your breathing whenever you remember.** Your breath is your anchor to bring you back to the present moment. If you're on the phone and find your mind keeps wandering, feel a few of your breaths to centre you in the present.

- ✔ **Record your progress.** Keep notes on what you complete in each hour to make you more mindful of your use of time. You can then begin to focus more effectively in each hour that you use.

Mindful leadership

A mindful leader values both inner reflection and outer action. Rather than reacting automatically to everyday challenges, mindful leaders ensure that they're consciously making the right decision with awareness, compassion and wisdom.

Mindful leadership does not mean that the leader is always practising mindful exercises and walking around in a Zen-like bubble! A mindful leader is very much a person of action, but understands the value of rest, reflection and renewal.

A mindful leader can make a positive difference to an organisation. Because they're better able to see the bigger picture rather than just immediate threats or opportunities, an organisation with mindful leaders can create solid corporate values and a clear mission statement.

Mindful leadership begins with self-awareness. These leaders are aware of their own thoughts, ideas, opinions, beliefs and emotional state, from moment to moment. Through this self-awareness, they can challenge their interpretations to discover new solutions. And through this self-awareness, they're better able to relate and communicate with others — they have high levels of emotional intelligence. (You'll find more about mindful leadership in Chapters 9 and 10.)

Some of the benefits of mindful leadership are hard to measure but easy to see. A mindful leader is more present, exudes a sense of control and makes their employees feel more cared for.

If you're in a leadership position, whether you manage 2 people or 2,000, try the following exercise to help you to be more mindful in just a few minutes:

1. **Practise a short mindful exercise.** Try mindfulness of breath for a few minutes (see Chapter 3).

2. **Spend a couple of minutes reflecting on your own state of mind.** Consider how you're feeling. What thoughts are popping into your mind?

3. **Think about your staff for a couple of minutes.** Consider what challenges they may be facing.

4. **Ask yourself: 'How can I best look after myself now?'**

5. **Ask yourself: 'How can I best look after my staff now?'**

Write down one idea for yourself and your staff, and, if appropriate, carry them out. The exercise combines mindfulness and compassion. The mindfulness part helps you to tune into your current state, and the support part is an act of self-compassion. Finally, considering ways of supporting others shows compassion and leads to staff feeling more valued. Looking after and appreciating staff can help you get far more from them than a pay rise or promotion.

Looking at the Organisational Benefits of Mindfulness

A mindful organisation is aware of and cares for its people, whether that's employees, volunteers, customers or suppliers — whoever they work with. The organisation understands the need to focus on revenue generation, but in the long rather than short term. The company is based on sound ethical and sustainable values; it aims to make a positive difference to the world. When hard decisions about discipline or redundancy are necessary, the organisation can make them but only after considering all other options. The organisation encourages physical exercise and good nutrition, mental wellbeing through mindfulness classes, and emotional wellbeing through social interaction and training. In order to get the best out of people, working hours are flexible, as are many of the working practices. The organisation celebrates success and fully engages staff when making major changes and decisions about the organisation's future. It helps staff to do more of what they really enjoy and to find meaning in their work in a way that benefits both the individual and organisation.

An unmindful organisation is highly short-term focused. It may want to increase its profits for this quarter rather than care for staff or customers. Its products or services may cause harm rather than provide value for its customers. Employees display a low level of interaction, communication and emotional intelligence because they work in a climate of fear. The wrong people are in the wrong positions and are unclear about their roles and responsibilities. Working hours are long and unsustainable, and the organisation frowns upon a healthy balance between work and home/social life. It doesn't respond effectively to changes taking place in its sector.

A mindful organisation may sound idealistic but high levels of workplace stress, burnout and inequality; lack of creativity;

unethical corporate behaviour; and too much short-term focus on profit mean that creating a mindful organisation isn't a luxury but an urgent necessity.

Happier, more engaged employees

One of our favourite business books is Tony Hsieh's *Delivering Happiness* (BusinessPlusUS, 2010). The author founded a company called Zappos in 1999. Zappos grew from zero sales in 1999 to $1 billion worth of sales in 2009. Hsieh says this success was the result of making customers happy — and he achieved that by making his employees happy.

Zappos has a set of 10 core values that the staff created together. They provide the foundation of the company's culture and are a guide to how to treat customers, suppliers, employees and sales reps in a mindful way. These values include:

- Creating fun and a little weirdness
- Being adventurous, creative and open-minded
- Pursuing growth and learning
- Building a positive team and family spirit
- Being passionate and determined

Happiness isn't usually a term bandied about in a workplace environment. Traditionally, if you wanted to increase productivity, you made employees work harder or attend a time management course, or looked for ways to automate tasks.

Mindfulness does make employees happy. So much so that the effects of happiness can be seen in brain scans! Happy people show greater activation in the left pre-frontal cortex. Completing an eight-week mindfulness course has resulted in employees demonstrating greater activity in that part of the brain — the mindfulness literally made them feel happier.

But so what? you may ask. It transpires that happiness is linked to a whole host of benefits in the workplace. Happier staff are more productive, creative, take fewer sick days and are more likely to be promoted. So good work doesn't make you happy but being happy creates good work.

Try the following tips to boost your happiness in the workplace using mindfulness. Share them!

✔ Spend two minutes practising mindfulness of breath (see Chapter 3), then write down three things about your workplace for which you're grateful.

✔ Go for a 15-minute mindful walk for every 1.5 hours of work you do. Successful master violinists were found to use this balance of work and rest to optimise their performance and wellbeing.

✔ Have a mindful conversation with the happiest colleagues at work. Happiness is contagious. If you're consciously present with happy colleagues at lunch, in your break or over a quick drink after work, you feel happier.

✔ Commit to doing at least one task really mindfully when at work. Start small and build up from there.

Greater creativity

How important do you think creativity is in your organisation? Is it important to innovate and find new ideas for products or services? Or do you simply keep doing the same thing and hope that your competitors won't catch up? Most people agree that, in the current economy, without innovation your competitors will soon overtake you. So, to be a successful organisation, you need your employees' brains to be as creative as possible. Creative solutions not only help your organisation, they also help to meet the needs of your customers.

Take a few moments to consider the stance of a creative brain — open, flexible, attentive and not too stressed. In fact, when you're in a mindful state, the creative part of your brain is activated.

Mindfulness creates the ideal conditions in your brain for creative thought. When you're unmindful, you're on auto-pilot, thinking the same old thoughts. When you're mindful, you're more awake, energised and aware of new ideas as they emerge.

Think back to the last time you had a creative idea. Were you feeling anxious or relaxed? Were you in the moment or mired in a fog of worries and concerns? Were you feeling happy or sad? Psychologist Mihaly Csikszentmihalyi draws on 30 years' experience of researching mindfulness to identify the following five stages when engaged in the creative process:

✓ **Preparation:** Immersion in an interesting problem that requires a creative solution.

✓ **Incubation:** A period of inner reflection.

✓ **Insight:** The 'Aha!' moment when the solution emerges.

✓ **Evaluation:** Deciding whether the solution can work.

✓ **Elaboration:** Turning the chosen solution into a final product.

Mindfulness comes into play in all the different stages but is most important in the second, incubation. In Figure 2-1, you can see how the often creative, unconscious brain struggles to offer new solutions because of a busy or negative mindset. When your mind is more open and calm through mindfulness, creative solutions can rise up into your unconscious brain.

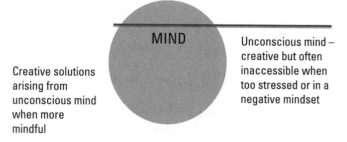

Figure 2-1: Diagram showing how mindfulness may work to increase your creative solutions.

Try the following exercises to boost your own creativity at work. Then share them with your colleagues to help you develop a more mindfully creative team.

1. **Become mindful of the problem.** Be crystal clear about what you're trying to solve. As Einstein said, 'If I had an hour to solve a problem I'd spend 55 minutes thinking about the problem and 5 minutes thinking about solutions.'

2. **Incubate.** Go for a mindful walk. Try practising mindfulness of breath (see Chapter 3). At home, take a bath and just enjoy the experience. Be in the moment rather than trying hard to solve the problem with your conscious mind. Let go. Allow things to be. Reflect.

3. **Collect solutions.** Come up with as many solutions as possible, no matter how weird or wacky. They may not work, but write them all down nonetheless. Allow ideas to flow from your mind to the sheet of paper. Be utterly non-judgemental as you compile this list.

4. **Evaluate.** Mindfully consider each solution in turn and analyse whether it would work. Avoid multi-tasking or other distractions. Take regular breaks as necessary. Being mindful at this stage means that your brain can work in optimal conditions to achieve success.

Increased productivity

Productivity isn't just about getting things done. Productivity is also about choosing what you need to do and doing those activities at a time of day when your energy levels and focus are highest.

Productivity is about working smarter, not just harder. There's nothing wrong with working hard when at work — being lazy at work doesn't lead to a fulfilling life or an effective organisation, sorry folks! But working smarter is about learning what you need to do and deciding how, when and where to do it.

Mindfulness improves focus. One of the direct benefits of greater focus is increased productivity. You stop being distracted by other thoughts, a text message or sounds in the office. Instead, you're able to keep your attention on whatever requires finishing.

Mindfulness of your own energy levels has a huge impact on productivity. As you become more mindful, you notice the subtle fluctuations in your energy levels. Noticing such things is an important skill. Everyone's energy rises and falls at different times of the day. When you recognise when your energy is at its peak, you can tackle your most challenging tasks. When your energy levels are naturally lower, you can use that time to chat with colleagues or take a break.

For example, if Gary knows that his energy levels peak in the morning and are lowest between 1 pm and 3 pm, he can make sure that he spends his time writing that important report in the office before anyone else arrives. In the afternoon, satisfied with a productive morning's work, he can call up his managers in London and catch up with progress over there.

Your energy levels also increase because you experience less emotional reactivity. Mindfulness increases your emotional awareness. So when you feel low, frustrated or angry, negative emotions don't creep up on you. You see the mood coming and you accept the feeling. You know that moods coming and going is part of being human. When something happens at work to make you feel upset or angry, you deal with your emotion before speaking. You express your emotions without losing control of yourself. This way of behaving is much more energy efficient, which means that you have energy left over to productively complete your work.

Practising mindfulness also gives you more energy because you worry less. Worrying causes your brain to use up 20 per cent of your energy, even though it comprises only 2 per cent of your body weight. Think back to the last time you spent a few minutes worrying — did you feel energised or drained afterwards? Most people feel drained. When you're mindful, you're more focused on the moment and what needs to be done, and you don't waste energy worrying. Remember, worry is like a rocking chair — it gives you something to do but never gets you anywhere. Mindfulness exercises help you to reduce your worrying.

Finally, by being mindful, your mind has the flexibility to step back to see the bird's eye view. Taking a quick overview means that you don't waste your time doing tasks that are unnecessary. Productivity isn't just about doing what needs doing, but also not doing what doesn't need doing!

Here are a few tips for making your organisation more productive:

- ✔ Dedicate a room to quiet time, mindfulness, prayer or meditation. Taking a break in this room gives staff time to reflect and recharge their batteries.

- ✔ Discourage working late. Working long hours reduces efficiency and productivity and has a negative impact on employees' home life, which inevitably affects their work life too.

- ✔ Encourage all staff to attend a mindfulness workshop and ensure that they have access to online courses, books or e-learning. Even a 1 per cent increase in productivity more than pays back the cost of the training and resources.

Improved decision-making

All CEOs know that high-quality decisions can make or break their organisation. When managers make effective decisions, staff work more efficiently, they feel more in control and the results can be seen in sustainable income for long-term growth.

You can make good decisions when your brain is functioning optimally. You can read all you like about decision theory, but if your brain isn't working optimally, you fail to take all factors into account and make bad decisions.

Think back to the last time you came home after a tough day at work. What sort of decisions did you make? Did you decide to eat a healthy fruit salad, go for a swim, practise mindfulness and phone a friend who needed cheering up? Or did you eat too much chocolate, slump in front of the TV and snap at your partner? The latter scenario is more likely — because your brain wasn't able to make good decisions. Your long-term goals of losing weight or being healthy or socialising more were overtaken by a brain starved of rest. This situation is called *decision fatigue*. The more decisions you make, without adequate breaks, the less effective your decisions will be. One way of countering decision fatigue is practising mindfulness exercises.

Another way in which mindfulness can help with decisions is by switching off the auto-pilot response in your brain. When operating without mindfulness, many of your decisions are automatic and based on previous decisions. They lack freshness and don't have access to any new information. If the employees of an organisation are more mindful, they can spot new ideas, see the activities of competitors, notice a need for new processes or consumers, and make a different decision — and thus move the company forward successfully.

For your day-to-day decisions, try the five-step approach shown in Figure 2-2.

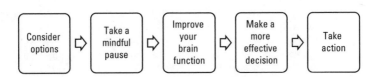

Figure 2-2: The process of mindful action.

By taking a mindful minute, or mindful pause (see Chapter 3), you can optimise your brain function, reduce decision fatigue and make better decisions.

Bear these tips in mind to improve your decision-making:

- ✔ Ensure that you schedule meetings at a time of day when people's energy levels are high, making mindful awareness more likely.

- ✔ If you're chairing a meeting, take a mindful pause before you start to ensure that you're in the right state of mind. End the meeting if you notice people's attention beginning to wane.

- ✔ Remember that you're a human being, not a machine. You can't keep making decisions all day and expect them to be of a high standard. Take a mindful break every 90 minutes, even if just for a minute.

Reducing staff turnover

High employee turnover hits the bottom line. The cost of replacing an employee and training them can cost up to twice that employee's salary. Consider the time involved in recruitment, for carrying out interviews as you screen candidates and the loss of productivity as the new employee learns the ropes. Maybe the new employee won't even work out and you then have to repeat the process. On top of that, constant changes of staff can negatively impact staff morale.

Mindfulness can help lower staff turnover by helping employees to cope better with stress. Stress can lead to illness and ultimately result in people being on long-term sick leave. But even for staff who aren't overwhelmed by stress, mindfulness can build their resilience and improve their performance, which will make them feel more valued.

Too much stress leads to burnout. According to Professor Marie Asberg, burnout is the end of an exhaustion funnel when you gradually stop doing things that you deem 'unimportant' such as exercising and socialising, and instead obsess about your workplace outcomes. Research carried out in 2009 found that doctors who practised mindfulness experienced decreased burnout rates.

Prevention is better than cure. Yet most organisations focus on fixing staff after they become ill rather than preventing stress-related illness in the first place. Most employers spend 200–300 per cent more on managing ill heath than on prevention.

Use the following mindful tips to help lower staff turnover:

- ✔ **Measure staff wellbeing and then implement means to improve it.** Search online for the 'University of Pennsylvania Authentic Happiness' website for lots of wellbeing questionnaires that you could try.

- ✔ **Set up a regular mindfulness group for all staff to attend for free in the workplace.**

- ✔ **Identify staff who may be susceptible to burnout.** Ensure that they have access to more regular mindfulness courses and other forms of help.

- ✔ **Train managers in mindfulness so they're better able to listen to their staff.** Being better listened to makes employees feel more cared for and they're less likely to leave the organisation as a result. Not being appreciated and listened to is one of the causes of high staff turnover.

- ✔ **Help employees to maintain a work-life balance.** A nationwide survey found that 20 per cent of employees left their job as a result of poor work-life balance and 20 per cent because of workplace stress. Mindfulness can help improve productivity so employees can get home earlier, thus improving their work-life balance and reducing their stress levels.

Chapter 3

Applying Mindfulness in the Workplace

*M*indfulness is all well and good, but how do you apply it effectively in the workplace? That's exactly what you find out in this chapter. You also discover why mindfulness is more important than ever in the modern workplace and find out lots of practical ways to start 'mindfulnessing' within minutes!

Gaining Perspective in the Modern-Day Workplace

Fifty years ago, a sizeable proportion of the population got a job and worked for that organisation until they retired. The key benefit resulting from this scenario was a sense of security and stability — you knew what to expect.

For students looking for a job today, things are very different. A recent survey of workers found that one in three remains in a job for less than two years. This massive change in people's working lives is bound to have an impact — sometimes positive, but often negative. In this section, we cover how mindfulness can help you deal with uncertainty in the workplace.

Applying mindfulness in changing times

The current rate of change in the workplace is faster than at any other time in history. The past 15 years have seen an explosion in communications technology and social networking, and a rapid rise in economic growth in the emerging economies of India, China, Russia and Brazil. These changes have a big impact on the workplace and affect employees at all levels. How can mindfulness help in managing these changes?

Change isn't always easy. Sometimes change in the workplace can be met with resistance. The human brain works through habit, which creates a sense of familiarity and security. Poorly managed change can make people feel threatened and they resist it.

Mindfulness is about being aware of the emotional impact of change. You need to prepare employees in advance, providing relevant training if necessary. Following the change, you must be a good listener and respond quickly if employees express frustration or distress.

A unique way of thinking about change is provided by a deeper understanding of the principles of mindfulness. Most mindfulness teaching stresses that the world is in a constant state of flux. Mindfulness exercises demonstrate this perpetual change. Try focusing on one of your senses for more than a few minutes and notice the variety of thoughts, feelings, bodily sensations and distractions that you experience.

The universe is constantly changing. Atoms are continually moving; in fact, scientists are unable to achieve absolute zero, the temperature at which atoms stop moving. If constant change is the way of the world, you need to expect some in your own life. Resisting that change leads to pain.

You need to expect and embrace the change that is bound to come. If you find yourself reacting with sadness or anger to that change, give yourself the time and space to work through those emotions using mindfulness exercises.

To better manage change in the workplace, try these tips:

✔ **Expect change:** If you're clinging to the hope that change won't happen, you're living with greater fear and anxiety. Instead, simply expect change to happen at work. When change doesn't happen, be pleasantly surprised.

✔ **Embrace change:** Try to see change as an opportunity. Write down the benefits of the change and view them as a chance to manage that change.

✔ **Anchor yourself in the present:** When you're faced with a torrent of change, you can easily feel flustered. One way of coping with that change is through mindfulness exercises. Even one deep breath taken mindfully can switch on your parasympathetic nervous system, which makes you more relaxed and grounded.

Change can be challenging. But in our experience, regular mindfulness practice makes managing external changes easier because you realise that, beyond your changing thoughts and emotions, a deeper sense of peace, calm and spaciousness exists that is simply your own awareness. That awareness is always the same, ever present and unchanging. When faced with too much change, you can take refuge in mindfulness to rest your body, mind and emotions in your own, unchanging awareness.

Building resilience

Facing too many challenges at work makes you feel overwhelmed and frustrated. In response you trigger your fight-or-flight mechanism. This threat response, if switched on for too long, leads to inefficient use of your brain and possibly disease in your body. Building resilience is a way of managing challenges more effectively. For more on mindfulness for resilience, see Chapter 4.

Take the example of Thomas Edison, legendary inventor of the light bulb. He famously said that each time he failed, he didn't view the experiment as a failure; rather he saw it as another way that didn't work. Seeing failed attempts as stepping stones to success is an example of a resilient attitude. Edison bounced back from attempts that didn't work to discover what did work. He certainly thrived on success, inventing the phonograph, motion picture and telegraph.

The achievements of Edison may seem hard to emulate. He seemed to be almost born with a positive attitude and destined for success. And, as far as we know, he didn't formally practise mindfulness! How can mindfulness help you?

As you become more mindful, your tendency to ruminate declines. *Rumination* is how much you think about and dwell on your problems. Rumination is like a broken record that keeps replaying itself — that argument you had with your colleague, that error you made in your presentation. If you ruminate, you overthink about situations or life events.

Mindfulness may be one of the most effective ways to reduce ruminative thinking because you become more aware of your thought patterns and more skilful at stepping back from unhelpful thoughts.

Mindfulness helps you to spot those little niggling negative thoughts before they grow too large. And mindfulness helps you to naturally see tough situations at work as challenges to be faced and overcome rather than avoided. If you're feeling overwhelmed by adversity, mindfulness won't offer a quick fix. But dealing with each challenge, step by step, combining mindfulness with help from your colleagues and/or a coach, means that you can begin to thrive at work.

Think of someone in your workplace who seems to thrive on change and whom you respect. Identify:

- ✔ His attitudes and beliefs
- ✔ The kind of language he uses to describe a change in the workplace
- ✔ The sort of hours he works and what he does to rest and recharge
- ✔ How mindful (present) he is when at work

Spending time talking with those who thrive on change in the workplace can help you to see things from their perspective.

Adjusting Your Mental Mindset

When Shamash discovered mindfulness, his mindset shifted 180 degrees. Before that first lesson in mindfulness, he was completely goal-orientated. He was halfway through a degree in chemical engineering and wanted a career working for a big corporation. He was only 20 years old, but ever since he was a boy he had striven to achieve the top grades at school so that he could get into a good university. He aimed to be among the best at university so that he could get a good job, and so on.

The obsessive desire for success was draining. But after that mindfulness class, something shifted. Shamash discovered that life was not only to be enjoyed in the future, after attaining all of your goals; life was to be enjoyed right now, here in the present moment. There's nothing wrong with achieving success and attaining goals, but not at the expense of the here and now. Ironically, by living in a more present-focused way, Shamash has been better able to achieve success — the best way to prepare for the future is to live in the present.

Everyone experiences being fully in the moment at some point. Consider the last time you were fully present at work — what were you doing? How did you feel? How productive were you?

Treating thoughts as mental processes

Some people estimate that they have up to 60,000 thoughts a day. If you've tried practising mindfulness exercises already, you probably think that's an underestimate. In the East, the brain's tendency to constantly go from one thought to another is called the 'monkey mind' because it resembles a monkey swinging from branch to branch.

Thoughts can be great. Through the power of thinking, humans have managed to achieve feats way beyond what any other animal on earth has done. We've created cities, designed planes and landed on the moon. Unfortunately, we've also designed nuclear weapons and heavily polluted the planet.

Thoughts have another disadvantage on a personal level too. If all your thoughts are taken to be true, and if those thoughts are self-critical, your mental wellbeing suffers. As a result, your performance at work declines too.

Try this thought bubble exercise:

1. **Picture bubbles floating away in the sky.** Maintain this image for one minute.

2. **Imagine that every thought you have can float away in one of those bubbles.**

3. **Let your mind wander.** Each time a thought pops into your head, imagine it drifting away in a bubble. Continue to do this for a few minutes. You may have lots of thoughts or very few. It doesn't matter.

How did you find this exercise? Did your thoughts float away? More importantly, were you able to observe your thoughts? If you were, you've demonstrated that you are not your thoughts — you can observe them from a distance.

The thought bubble and similar exercises help to show you an important mindfulness skill: The ability to step back from your thoughts. You may have all sorts of thoughts popping into your head in the workplace, such as:

- ✔ I'm useless in meetings.

- ✔ I can't handle this project. It's too big for me.

- ✔ What if Mike tells Michelle about my report? I'll miss my chance at promotion.

- ✔ I hate working with David. He's too slow for me.

These types of thoughts have an effect on your emotions, bodily sensations and ability to get your work done.

Mindfulness offers a solution. As you become more mindful, you notice these thoughts more often. You're then able to step back from them, seeing them as mental processes in your mind rather than absolute truths.

Being able to step back from your thoughts takes practice, especially in the hustle and bustle of the workplace. For this reason, we recommend that you try out some of these exercises when you're not under too much pressure. Once your brain gets the hang of how to watch and step back from unhelpful thoughts, you have a powerful and life-changing skill.

In the old days of personal development, self-help gurus promoted 'positive thinking'. For most people, slapping positive thoughts on top of negative beliefs means they just slip off. Instead, you need to become aware of those negative beliefs and see them for what they are — just thoughts.

Use the following exercise to deal with your thoughts and mind state when you're judging things negatively. It's a simple process but has long-lasting effects once it becomes a habit for you.

You can deal with your negative thoughts by following these three simple steps:

   1. **Notice your thoughts:** Focus particularly on unhelpful thoughts about yourself, others or your workplace.

2. **Step back from your thoughts:** See them as simply mental processes arising in your mind that aren't necessarily true. You can imagine them on clouds, in bubbles or floating away like leaves on a stream. The idea is to create a sense of distance between you and your thoughts — not to just get rid of them.

3. **Refocus your attention on the task or person in front of you:** The more mindfulness exercises you practise, the better your brain gets at dealing with negative thoughts.

Approaching rather than avoiding difficulties

Say that work causes you anxiety. You worry about all the meetings you have to attend, the deadlines you have to meet and the colleagues you have to deal with. How do you cope with that feeling of anxiety? Should you continue to face up to the challenges at work and just get on with the uncomfortable feeling of anxiety, or should you avoid anything that makes you feel that way?

You can avoid the feeling by working even harder so that your attention is completely focused on the task in hand and not on your anxiety. Or you can go for a drink every evening after work, causing the emotional sensation to reduce. Or you can start eating every time that feeling arises, so your attention is focused on the food instead of your anxiety.

All these strategies help you to avoid the feeling of anxiety in the workplace. Unfortunately, however, none of them work over the long term. The feeling of anxiety is still there and requires an increasing number of avoidant strategies to help you suppress it.

Mindfulness is about approach rather than avoidance. It helps you to approach unpleasant feelings at a pace that's right for you.

Approaching difficult emotions when you've always found a way to avoid them isn't easy at first. To help you get better at doing so, you need to approach your feelings as you'd approach a kitten. You don't rush towards a kitten because it gets frightened and runs away. You approach a kitten slowly. First you walk towards it and then you crouch down so that you don't look too big. Next, you reach out and gently stroke it. Hopefully, the kitten begins to trust you and eventually you can pick it up.

Treat whatever emotion you're dealing with in the same way. Notice where you're holding the feeling in your body. Approach the feeling slowly and tentatively, with a sense of curiosity. Gradually you come to fully feel the sensation, just as it is. This experience is like having a kitten in your hand. Unlike a kitten, however, the feeling is likely to change as you approach it.

Sometimes it grows, sometimes it dissolves. But that's not the point. The point is that you're *willing* to feel that emotion and approach rather than avoid it. This empowering move leads to greater emotional regulation — you have control over your emotion rather than the emotion controlling you.

Approaching emotions involves a process of non-judgemental acceptance — a key aspect of mindfulness. When you're practising mindfulness, you're endeavouring to experience thoughts, emotions, sensations and events as they are in the moment, without trying to judge them as good or bad, desirable or undesirable.

Approach a challenge rather than avoid it, if you can, and discover how to accept the sensations that it produces. Being able to approach your difficulties makes you feel more confident and you're less likely to let your emotions control your life.

Rewiring your brain

Your brain is made up of neurons, which are like wires that carry electrical current from one place to another. Each neuron is connected to many others. The brain is the most complex organism in the known universe and scientists still have very little idea about how it works.

If you were at school in the 1970s, you were probably taught that your brain gradually deteriorates as you get older. The prevailing view was that the brain can't improve itself and that neurons die off as you age. That view was incorrect! We now know that you can create new connections in your brain at any age.

Your brain is unique and shaped by your daily experiences and what you pay attention to. If you're a violinist, the part of your brain that maps touch in your fingers is actually larger. If you're a taxi driver in New York, the part of your brain responsible for spatial awareness is more pronounced. And if you're a mindfulness practitioner, the area of your brain that controls focus is more powerful, as is the part that manages emotions. If you're a mindfulness practitioner, the area of the brain responsible for higher levels of wellbeing is more active — the left prefrontal cortex.

An explosion of interest in the study of mindfulness has recently occurred. Centres for mindfulness have been established at numerous universities all over the world.

Throughout this book we share insights about the effects of mindfulness on the brain. In this section we describe findings from the world of *neuroscience*.

Re-sculpting your brain to make you more productive at work

Most people feel that their mind is all over the place. In fact, some people who practise mindfulness even think that the exercises make them less focused! Studies show that the opposite is actually true. When you sit down to be mindful, you're much more likely to notice each time your mind gets distracted. Usually, your mind is even less focused — so much so that you don't even realise it.

Brain scans reveal that even after just a week or so of daily mindfulness practice, the parts of the brain dedicated to paying attention (which include the parietal and prefrontal structures), become more activated. In other words you're actively improving your brain's ability to pay attention. Longer-term practitioners appear to have more permanent changes in the brain, showing a greater propensity to be in the present moment even when in a resting state.

In his most recent book, *Focus*, psychologist Daniel Goleman argues that incessant use of technology, such as emails and text messages, has rendered young people increasingly distracted. He goes on to say that current research suggests that mindfulness exercises enable the brain to rewire itself and become more focused.

Goleman identifies three types of focus that are required for different types of tasks:

> ✔ **Concentration:** Focusing on one thing only and blocking out distractions — ideal for completing tasks requiring your full attention.

✔ **Open presence:** You are receptive to all incoming information — ideal if you're in a leadership position that requires you to see the big picture and identify how all the different activities help the organisation achieve its goals.

✔ **Free association:** Letting go of your old ideas and allowing your mind to drift — ideal when tapping into your creativity.

Mindfulness directly helps to strengthen the networks in your brain associated with concentration and open presence, and allows you to choose to engage in free association when you need to.

Using mindfulness to increase your present-moment circuitry

Children love stories. Adults love stories. Have you ever wondered why? The brain is designed to be hooked by stories. Stories switch on the visual part of your brain. Because stories are formed of connecting ideas, they tune into the connections in your own brain.

Some people refer to the brain as a storytelling machine. Think about when you first wake up in the morning. Your mind is blank and then, suddenly, whoosh! Who you are and where you live and that long to-do list come to mind.

Your storytelling mind is the 'default' network in your brain. In other words, your brain's normal mode is to tell you stories about yourself and others. For example, 'I need to finish this project by noon, then I need to have a chat with Paul before I get dressed to meet my editor. I must make sure that I'm on time. That hotel we're meeting in looks very big. I hope we can find a table. I wonder if my co-author can join us . . .?'

That's the storytelling brain at work — not always terribly exciting and often repetitive. But mindfulness is different and much more interesting. If your brain is in a more mindful state, you're focused on the present moment, which engages a different circuitry in your brain. You can access the present moment right now by noticing the sensations that your body is experiencing as it sits on a chair. Do you start to become aware of your poor posture or notice tension in your neck? You can now start to notice information from the world around you: The coolness of the book you're holding, the size of the tree outside, the wispy clouds and hints of a blue sky beyond. That's present-focused attention.

When you're more present-moment focused, rather than running on your default network all the time, you're more in control of your life. Instead of finding yourself aimlessly surfing the internet, you can catch yourself and choose to get on and finish your work. If you're lost in thought after thought, you can't make a choice about what you're doing until you snap out of the dream. Mindfulness offers you that choice.

Balance is the secret to success. Combining one longer period of mindfulness with short mindful exercises throughout the day makes you a mindfulness-at-work superstar!

Fitting Mindfulness into Your Day

It's a common misconception that the only way to practise mindfulness is to sit down, close your eyes and focus for a period of time. In reality there are lots of ways to weave in mindfulness throughout your day. In the next section you will discover some easy ways to integrate mindfulness into your day, both at home and at work.

Starting the day mindfully

The way you start your morning often sets the tone for the rest of your day. If you make a positive start with a short mindful exercise, you're off to a conscious, perhaps calmer, start. You're then more likely to be able to maintain mindful awareness throughout the day.

Waking up too late every day, not stopping even for a moment to be in the present, makes your life more difficult. Rushing releases a burst of adrenaline into your bloodstream, narrowing your brain's attentional resources. You're much more likely to see others as annoying threats to your goal of getting to work on time — little mindfulness is evident in that state of mind. You're then probably running on automatic for most of the day, having used up a lot of your energy just getting to work and, before you know it, the day has ended and you're feeling shattered. If this scenario sounds familiar, don't worry. Discover a different way of starting your day in this section.

Here is an example of a mindful morning routine. Feel free to adjust it depending on your lifestyle, responsibilities and preferences.

✔ **5.30 am — You wake up naturally.** You used to need an alarm clock, but because you now go to bed at a reasonable time, you wake up on time too. You therefore wake up after a good night's sleep. You begin the day with a few mindful breaths and a smile as you prepare to get up.

✔ **5.31 am — You have a short morning stretch, perhaps do a few mindful yoga exercises and then prepare yourself a cup of tea.** You listen to the sound of the kettle boiling and notice the steam rising. You begin reflecting on all the aspects of your life that you're grateful for. You enjoy the sound of water filling your mug of lemon and ginger tea.

✔ **5.45 am — You sit down facing your garden and spend a few minutes looking out of the window and sipping your tea.** You then practise a mindfulness exercise for 10 minutes. You finish by describing your experience in your journal and noting three things you're grateful for in your life.

✔ **6.00 am — You wake up the children to let them know it's time to get ready for school.** They're a bit groggy but you've more patience since you started practising mindfulness. They know the routine and before too long they're dressed and ready to go. Your partner helps to get them prepared for school. You remember how grateful you are to have such lovely children.

✔ **7.00 am — You have breakfast together as a family.** Before eating, your youngest child says, 'Let's mindfully pause' and you all take three mindful breaths together. You eat and talk about the day to come and everyone shares how they're feeling and what's on their mind. As best you can, you eat with mindful awareness. You remind your children to look for the good things in the day, so you can share them that evening.

✔ **7.30 am — You all leave the house together.** You've enough time to travel mindfully to work.

We know this scenario may sound hopelessly optimistic. The purpose of this description is to help you find one or two ideas that you can implement in your life. Begin with where you are at the moment. Try going to bed a little earlier and waking up a bit earlier. Spend a few moments deliberately thinking about what's going well in your life as a positive way to start the day.

Travelling mindfully

A Gallup poll of over 170,000 people revealed that commuting to work is the least enjoyable of daily activities. Longer commutes are correlated with higher divorce rates, obesity, decreased exercise and higher consumption of fast foods. A third of those with journeys of over 90 minutes had chronic neck or back pain issues. But, if you have a long commute, don't despair!

These findings suggest that identifying ways to make travel more mindful can have a significant effect on people's health, happiness, relationships, productivity and work success. Use this section to make travelling more tolerable, and perhaps even fun!

Driving with intent

Here are a few tips for making your car journeys more mindful:

- ✔ **Start the journey with mindfulness.** By grounding yourself with a mindfulness practice, you set the tone for your journey.

- ✔ **Keep to the speed limit.** Even if the road is empty and you think that you can safely drive faster, don't. Driving a little slower than you're used to means that you're able to dedicate more of your brain's resources to driving with mindful awareness.

- ✔ **Expect delays.** Expect delays, traffic, learner drivers and more traffic. Then, if you have a smooth journey to work, you can be pleasantly surprised rather than frustrated.

- ✔ **Switch off your phone.** Lots of research has demonstrated that using a phone while driving, even if the phone is hands-free, impairs driving ability to the same extent as drinking too much alcohol.

- ✔ **Be mindful of your surroundings.** Mindful driving is about maintaining an open awareness. Look both near and far to help you judge any dangers coming up. See driving as an opportunity to practise mindfulness.

- ✔ **End mindfully.** When you arrive at work, finish with another little mindful exercise, such as mindfulness of breath, mindfulness of sounds, or mindfulness of your body. Continue this process by walking with mindful awareness to your workplace rather than zoning out.

Trains

If you commute on the train every day, you can do so mindfully so that you arrive at work focused rather than frazzled.

Here are a few tips to help you be mindful on the train:

- ✔ **Practise a mindfulness exercise.** Pop on headphones and practise a guided mindfulness exercise during your journey.

- ✔ **Expect delays.** Don't expect the service to be perfect. That way you'll be pleasantly surprised if it goes smoothly and not too frustrated if things go wrong.

- ✔ **Count the sounds.** A game you can play on the train is to notice all the different types of sounds you can hear. You'll probably be surprised by all the different tones of sound that you normally ignore.

- ✔ **Pay attention.** Notice what's going on around you on the train. Watch the other passengers; observe the kinds of things they're doing and what they're wearing. Try to observe without judging. Most people focus their attention on a book, a newspaper or music. Try something different — open up and look with curiosity at the world around you.

Planes

Several of Shamash's clients regularly use mindfulness practices when they're on long-haul flights and swear that they no longer suffer from jet lag.

Sitting in a confined space for hours can be frustrating. If you can't sleep, what do you do? Practising mindfulness is a great idea in this situation.

- ✔ **Identify your triggers.** Which specific aspect of the flight are you scared of?

- ✔ **Familiarise yourself with the noises.** Avoid panic by knowing a little about how a plane takes off, flies and lands.

- ✔ **Sip herbal tea mindfully.** Drinking in a mindful way, conscious of the taste and aroma, makes you feel more relaxed and in control.

✔ **Use drugs as a last resort.** If you've been given medication to manage your anxiety, see whether you can use other mindfulness techniques first. (*Note:* Obviously, your doctor's advice should take precedence over whatever we suggest.)

✔ **Breathe through your anxiety**. If you feel anxious, mindful deep breathing is helpful. Begin by breathing out for as long as you can and then draw a slow, deep breath in. Focusing fully on the sensation of breathing helps to anchor you in the present so that you can't ruminate on negative thoughts.

Taking mindful pauses

A mindful pause is simply a chance to stop and practise a short mindfulness exercise. People love the short mindful exercises that we offer when we're running a workshop or coaching session. The thought of a two-minute mindful exercise puts a smile on their faces.

We recommend that you do several short mindful exercises per day rather than one long mindfulness session. We suggest this approach because mindfulness is about being more present and awake in your everyday life — at work and at home. If you practise regularly, this result is more likely to happen.

Pausing at your desk

A mindful pause isn't a relaxation break. Relaxation can often be not only about letting go of muscular tension but also allowing the mind to drift freely. A mindful pause is about gently waking up — noticing thoughts, feelings and bodily sensations rather than tuning them out.

One of the challenges of mindfulness is remembering to practise. Use the following tips to remind you to do a mindful pause:

✔ Pause between activities.

✔ Set a reminder on your phone. Set periodic alarms on your phone to remind you to pause.

✔ Use a phone app to remind you to stop and take a breath or two.

> ✔ Make an appointment with yourself. Use a diary to remind you to stop and take a few mindful pauses.
>
> ✔ Be creative. Consider your work role and how you can creatively remind yourself to take a mindful break or three.

Waking up and smelling the coffee

Another way to take a subtle mindful pause is when you go on your coffee break.

Most people let their minds have free rein and drift. But the problem with allowing this drift too often is that the mind goes to the same old worries and concerns. Tune in rather than out to fully recharge yourself.

Follow these steps:

1. **Set aside time for your break so that you can enjoy a mindful drink.**

2. **Be mindful as you prepare your drink.** Listen to the sound of the boiling water, watch the steam, smell the aroma and listen to the sound of water filling your cup.

3. **Sit down with your drink and switch off any potential distractions.** Choose a location where you're unlikely to be disturbed.

4. **Breathe mindfully.** Feel your breath, your body and the cup in your hands.

5. **Take a sip of your drink.** Feel the warmth of the liquid entering your mouth and going down your throat. Continue to hold the cup and watch the steam rising from it. Feel your breathing from time to time.

6. **Notice the tendency to rush or finish.** Take your time and let the temptation to rush arise and pass, like any other feeling.

7. **Express gratitude when you finish drinking.** Show appreciation for this opportunity to practise mindfulness.

If you work in a busy environment, taking this length of time over a drink may not be possible. Modify the exercise in accordance with your needs. Stopping for 60 seconds to really taste your drink can make a big difference to your mindset in that moment.

Ending your day mindfully

Ending your working day with mindfulness helps to set boundaries. You signal to your brain that you've now stopped work — you can shift gear from the busy, *doing* mode to a more mindful *being* mode.

Creating boundaries

Creating a boundary between your work and home life is key. Consider practising a mindfulness exercise as soon as you're off work and at home. This signals to your brain that work time is over and you can shift mental gears and begin to relax and rejuvenate. Try to avoid checking your emails in the evening. To become more mindful, you need to set aside time to do something different and reset your brain so you're recharged for the next day. If you're checking your work emails after your workday is done and just can't help it, you may be addicted to doing so. This type of addiction is more common than you think. Check out Chapter 5 for more on technology addiction.

Following a mindful evening routine

Your routine evening activities are a great opportunity to be extra mindful. You can be mindful when you cook, do the ironing, mow the lawn, vacuum and so on. These household chores are normally thought of as repetitive and boring — mindfulness allows you to see them in a different light.

Here's a list of a few typical evening activities and ways to make them more mindful after a busy day at work:

- ✔ **Watching television:** If you're stuck in the habit of watching several hours of television each night, try keeping a journal of your TV habits — the act of writing them down can help you to shift the habit.

- ✔ **Cooking:** Cooking is a great opportunity to practise mindfulness. Connect with your senses as you cook.

- ✔ **Eating:** Really notice and appreciate every element of your meal. Use all of your senses to enhance the experience.

- ✔ **Doing sport or exercise:** These activities can be good for more than just your body, they are a great opportunity for practising mindfulness too.

- ✔ **Enjoying a hobby:** Hobbies are great for taking your mind off work. Any hobby or activity can be mindful.

Sleep is important. A good night's sleep has a positive effect on energy levels, willpower, general wellbeing, and the ability to communicate and focus. Studies suggest that you need 7.5 to 9 hours' sleep per night to operate at your optimum level. The exact figure varies from one person to the next. Mindfulness will probably help you to sleep better too. And if you can't sleep, try a mindfulness exercise when you're in bed. Mindfulness is restful and should help you drift off.

Avoid looking at any form of screen in the last couple of hours before going to sleep. The light from screens sends a signal to your brain that it's still daytime and makes it harder for you to fall asleep because it lowers your levels of melatonin.

Developing Your Mindfulness Practice

This section describes some of the key principles of true mindfulness, which are important both in the workplace and beyond. Some of these principles have emerged from ancient practices, developed by millions of people over thousands of years. Take a few moments to consider the key aspects of mindfulness at work and whether these ideas resonate with you. The end of this chapter also outlines some key mindfulness practices, and the free MP3 downloads that we have prepared to help you develop your own mindfulness practice.

Examining your attitude

Your attitudes are also important. Jon Kabat-Zinn, co-developer of mindfulness-based approaches in the West, recommends developing the following attitudes to life.

Being non-judgemental

Your mind is constantly judging experiences as good or bad. Mindfulness practice offers time for you to let go of those internal judgements and just observe whatever you're experiencing, accepting the moment as it is.

Being patient

Mindfulness requires patience. You need to bring your attention back to the present again and again. If you're naturally impatient, mindfulness is probably the best training you can undertake!

Adopting a beginner's mind

If you adopt a beginner's mind, you undertake each mindfulness practice as if the experience was a completely new one. To work with a beginner's mind means that you approach your work with freshness as if you've never done that kind of work before. Adopting this attitude helps you to switch off your habitual, automatic ways of doing things.

Being accepting

Acceptance is a fundamental aspect of mindfulness. To accept means to stop fighting with your present-moment experience and just be aware of whatever is happening. For example, if you feel discomfort in your body when you're practising mindfulness, and shifting your posture doesn't ease it, just acknowledge the sensation and let it be.

Letting go

When Shamash was writing his first book, he struggled. He wanted it to be perfect. But the more he strove for that, the longer the book took to write. When Shamash finally let go of the idea of perfection, the words began to flow. Letting go was the key. Letting go is an act of freedom. When you let go of old ideas, beliefs, people, jobs or ways of working, you create space for the new. When practising mindfulness, you need to let go of each stream of thought that you notice. The process is a continuous movement of observation and letting go.

Remembering that practice makes perfect

Monks practise mindfulness for years. Early scientific research into mindfulness investigated the effect it has on monks. Brain scans revealed that monks' brains operate far more effectively than those of people who don't practise mindfulness. The researchers also found that the more practice a monk had undertaken, the greater number of positive changes observed. Monks have an incredible ability to focus, they can manage their emotions very well, they experience lots of positive emotions (that's why they're always smiling!) and rarely, if ever, lose their temper.

The good news is you don't need to become a monk to benefit from mindfulness. Positive changes have been observed in the brains of people who've been practising mindfulness for just 10–20 minutes a day for a few days.

Daily practice is the key. Consider the process of discovering how to ride a bike. If you spend just one minute a day practising, you eventually get better but doing so takes years! If you practise for 20 minutes a day with a teacher, you may be able to ride within a week or two. Once you get the hang of riding a bike, to be able to cycle faster you need regular practice. You may need to train with a coach, read books about cycling, meet other cyclists to share ideas, and so on. Mindfulness is similar. You need to practise regularly, and the more time you can dedicate to being mindful, the better you get at it. You can start slowly with short mindful exercises and gradually build up to longer sessions. If you want to get really good at mindfulness, you need to read about it, get a coach or trainer and practise diligently.

Key mindfulness practices

The following practices are available as audio downloads from www.dummies.com/go/mawessentials. Try them yourself. You might pick one a week, and practice it for a full week, once or twice each day. Alternatively you might want to experiment with trying out different ones each day. Remember that all of these practices are straightforward and easy to learn, but do take some effort to master. Approach each of them with a 'beginner's mind', letting go of expectations of success and failure. As mindfulness teacher and author Jon Kabat-Zinn puts it, 'You don't have to like it, you just have to do it!'

Mindfulness of breath

One of the core skills of mindfulness is being able to direct your attention at will to where you want it to be. Sounds easy? Most people find this simple task really difficult at first.

This exercise uses the breath as an anchor point on which to focus your attention. The reason we use breath is that breath is universal — everyone breathes! In this exercise, make sure that you do not try to control your breath, just observe it.

The exercise isn't about relaxing (although many people do find it so). Rather, the exercise is about 'falling awake' — becoming more aware of what's happening in your mind. Think of yourself as a kind scientist, inquisitively observing everything that's going on without judging or categorising it.

Mindfulness of Breath is Track 1 of the audio downloads available at www.dummies.com/go/mawessentials, which guides you through the exercise.

The body scan

The body scan is all about getting back in touch with your body. Your body has more of an impact on your mind than you may expect. Mindfulness of your body sensations encourages you to shift into approach mode rather than work in avoidance mode. When practising the body scan you slowly move up your body from your toes to your scalp, focusing on each area of the body in turn.

A guided, audio version of this exercise is available (Track 2) at www.dummies.com/go/mawessentials.

Three-step body check

This version of the body scan can be done anywhere, as long as you have a chair, about three minutes to spare, and are unlikely to be disturbed. It's quick and easy to do at your desk.

Follow the instructions in the audio download available on www.dummies.com/go/mawessentials (Track 3).

Mindful walking

Mindful walking is about being present as you're walking, rather than letting your mind just aimlessly drift to other thoughts or things you need to do.

You can practise mindful walking in lots of different ways. You can walk slow or fast, focusing your attention on the present-moment sensations of walking. Listen to Track 4 of the audio downloads that you can find at www.dummies.com/go/mawessentials. We suggest that you practise this technique slowly at home and then, when you've got the hang of it, you can mindfully walk at your normal pace when you're at work. Try this exercise for five to 10 minutes to start with.

Chapter 4

Boosting Your Mental Resilience

*W*e all go to work to do a good job, and I'm sure that you're no exception. Unfortunately, the world of work can be challenging, which can make it difficult for you to perform at your best.

Change is the most common source of pressure at work. In the world of work, change is nothing new. In fact, you can argue that change is the only constant in life. What is different nowadays is that the pace of change is accelerating; uncertainty and instability are the norm in today's work environment.

Other sources of pressure you may encounter in the workplace include relationships with colleagues and peers, lack of clarity about job roles, work demands, degree of control over work, and support from colleagues and superiors.

This chapter explores how you can overcome work challenges by using mindfulness to boost your mental resilience. You find out how mindfulness can help you deal with work challenges more productively, leaving you with more energy and a sense of wellbeing. You discover strategies to help you flourish in times of change, managing multiple, conflicting demands more effectively. You develop a more mindful approach to encounters with difficult colleagues and bosses.

Recognising the Need for Resilience at Work

Resilience is all about your capacity to handle difficulties, demands and high pressure without becoming stressed. It's about not wasting energy on little things that really aren't important. It's about performing well under pressure. It's your ability to respond flexibly and adapt to changing circumstances (especially important in the present climate of constant change and uncertainty). Lastly, it's about your ability to bounce back from defeat and disaster.

The more resilient you are, the more quickly you will be able to recover from a setback, make the best of the new situation, and become a 'new and improved' version of yourself. From a business perspective, it's a no-brainer: A resilient workforce is a productive workforce. It's healthy, energetic, durable and enthusiastic — good news for both you and your company.

The modern-day stress epidemic

Unfortunately most of the world is now facing a stress epidemic. Take, for example, Bob, a busy account manager who works for a multinational company. As Bob's workload increases he starts to think, 'There's so much to do and not enough time.' This anxiety leads to him making poor decisions. As a result of his poor decisions, he starts to worry about his professional reputation, and the possibility of losing his job. Bob really wanted to shine at work, so he decides to work harder, putting in long hours. He becomes stressed, and makes more mistakes, so he starts taking work home. He gets stuck in a vicious cycle of worrying, working too hard and feeling stressed.

The end result? The harder he works, the more he gets wrong and the more stressed he feels. Does this scenario sound familiar?

Everyone, at some point in their working lives, experiences stress. Work-related stress can be defined as 'an adverse reaction to excessive pressures or demands'. Workplace stress is common; indeed, in many countries workplace stress is the top cause of long-term workplace absence. It costs businesses billions. In the UK alone, in 2012 around 131 million days were lost to sickness absence.

More people than ever before say that they feel highly stressed. As many as 80 per cent of workers say they regularly experience stress at work, and up to 40 per cent say that their job is very or extremely stressful and is the number one stressor in their lives. Estimates suggest that around 50 per cent of staff say that they need help in finding out how to manage stress.

Understanding fight or flight

So, if change is the norm, and stress is reaching epidemic proportions, how can you become more resilient? How can you bring joy and happiness back to your day, not to mention improved productivity and personal effectiveness?

To answer these questions, you first have to understand a little bit about how the human brain has evolved. Scientists think that in ancient times, when our ancestors were faced with a threat (such as attack by a wild animal), their brain triggered the release of powerful hormones into the bloodstream. These hormones boosted their heart rate, muscle tension and breathing, and helped them to sprint away from danger — the *fight-or-flight* response. Other hormones worked as natural painkillers, repaired damaged cells and acted as clotting agents. Together, the effect of these hormones helped humans to escape mortal danger and live to hunt another day. After the immediate threat had passed, our ancestors' bodies probably returned to normal fairly quickly.

Your own brain's reaction to modern-day pressures (such as a critical boss, a failed pitch, a missed promotion or a missed mortgage payment) is exactly the same as that of your ancestors. When you feel threatened, your brain releases an excessive amount of hormones, which are designed to help you escape from mortal danger.

Under normal circumstances, when you're not under any great pressure, and you experience a threat, a temporary spike in your heart rate occurs as hormones are released. After the perceived 'danger' has passed, your body returns to normal. Unfortunately, many people now live their lives in a constant state of heightened arousal.

The human ability to recognise and quickly react to perceived threats has helped us become highly successful as a species, but is now a danger to our very survival. Mindfulness can help you develop resilience to life's pressures, and new strategies for dealing with potential stressors in a more productive and less harmful manner, returning your body to a fit, healthy state.

Mindful Working to Enhance Resilience

Work is, and has always been, challenging. The digital age, constant change and the need for ever more efficient, cost-effective ways of working has led to some unhealthy working practices.

Managing multiple, conflicting demands

Do you spend your working life juggling multiple tasks and conflicting demands? If so, you're not alone. As people take on more senior roles, they're increasingly expected to multi-task — to work simultaneously on a range of different problems. For decades now, job descriptions have demanded the ability to multi-task.

The only way to do two or more mental tasks quickly and accurately is to consciously do one at a time. The only exception to this rule is routine tasks that you've done many times before. As a result, they've become embedded deep within the more primitive areas of your brain. In order to manage multiple, conflicting demands more productively, you need to plan your approach mindfully.

Managing tasks mindfully

Mindfulness can help you to become more aware of your mental processes, and choose the most appropriate strategy to deal with the work tasks you're facing.

Meet Jan. It's February and Jan has just been promoted to chief editor for an alternative lifestyle magazine. Jan starts her day by working through her emails. She reads, replies to and deletes messages. A couple of the emails prompt her to do some work. Two hours later she still hasn't started work on the editorial for this month's magazine, and the deadline is the end of the day. Jan starts working on the editorial, but she finds it difficult to focus. After 30 minutes, she's interrupted by Frank who is working on a feature for next month's magazine. She helps Frank, and then refocuses her attention on her editorial. Because she feels pressed for time, she eats a sandwich at her desk for lunch while trying hard to finish her editorial. In the afternoon, she chairs an important meeting about a feature in the Christmas edition. She hasn't had time to prepare and feels uncomfortable throughout the meeting. The meeting overruns. The time is now 4 pm and she still hasn't completed her editorial. Jan tries to focus but just can't think straight . . .

Have you had days like this? I certainly have! So what could Jan have done differently? Let's rewind Jan's day and look at how she could have made her life easier:

Jan entered the office. She knew that she'd face multiple, conflicting demands, so she decided to start her day mindfully with 10 minutes of mindfulness practice in her office before people came in. She started her day by prioritising all the things she had to do.

She identified that her editorial was the most important thing that day. In order to complete this task she knew she needed to use her higher brain (refer to Chapter 1), which is very powerful, but also very energy-hungry. This prompted her to undertake this task early on in the day while still feeling fresh. Frank popped in to ask for help, and she agreed to talk to him in the late afternoon. She completed her editorial by 11 am and then started working through her emails. She felt herself becoming distracted by a couple of emails that demanded her attention. Jan decided to go out for lunch. On her walk to the sandwich shop, she spent five minutes mindfully walking. She sat on a park bench to eat her sandwich, and spent a few moments mindfully savouring its taste and texture. She returned to the office feeling refreshed, with a clear head. She then spent 30 minutes, as planned at the start of the day, preparing for her meeting. The meeting was a great success, and finished early. She completed the work connected with the emails, helped Frank and left the office early.

Mindfulness helped Jan to acknowledge and park all the things that were going around in her head. It also helped her to regain her focus at lunchtime. By prioritising, she got more done in less time.

In the next section we cover a quick mindfulness technique that you can use any time you want to regain your focus.

Using the three-step focus break

This simple technique consists of doing three things for one minute each:

- ✔ Acknowledging your thoughts
- ✔ Focusing on the present-moment sensation of breathing
- ✔ Acknowledging your bodily sensations

Step 1: Settle yourself into a comfortable, upright position with your feet firmly on the floor — avoid slouching if you can. Although you can do this exercise with your eyes open, most people find it easier with closed eyes. By closing your eyes, your brain has one less stimulus to deal with. Spend one minute recognising and acknowledging all the thoughts going around in your head. As thoughts arise, acknowledge them, and then let them go.

Step 2: Narrow your attention to focus on the present-moment sensation of breathing. Feel the breath coming in and the breath going out. If your mind wanders, that's fine — it's just what minds do. Kindly, gently escort your attention back to where it needs to be. Remember, there is no need to control your breathing or alter it in any way. It's fine as it is — all you're doing is using it as a kind of anchor to direct your attention to.

Step 3: Spend one minute recognising and acknowledging how your body feels, right here and now. Become aware of the actual physical sensations in your body, including both the pleasant and unpleasant feelings. If you do encounter any unpleasant sensations, try if you can to just accept that they are there without trying to make them go away and without judging them as being bad or irritating. Doing so will evoke an emotion that will increase your tension and make things worse. Accept the sensations as they are in the present moment and accept that they won't add further fuel to the fire. As a result, the sensations may diminish or change.

This technique can be compressed or extended and can be used anywhere at any time. Creating a short break helps you return to the present moment. Returning to the present moment enables you to put things into perspective, see the bigger picture, make wiser choices and decide how to get the most from the rest of the day.

You may find this exercise difficult at first, but with a little practice it should become easier. Practising this technique helps you to develop new neural pathways in your brain, or strengthen existing ones. The stronger the neural pathways are, the easier it is to recall and repeat the exercise in future. Refer to Chapter 1 for more on neuroplasticity.

Here are a few tips to help you master the three-step focus break:

- ✔ Don't judge, rationalise or think about your thoughts, as doing so shifts you towards left-brain (logical) thinking. Just acknowledge that the thoughts are there and label them 'mental processes'. You may initially find this process difficult but it becomes easier with practice.

- ✔ Don't get cross if your mind wanders, as this wandering may start a rush of neurotransmitters signalling a response similar to fight or flight, which is not what you're aiming to do! If you do find yourself getting annoyed, be nice to yourself by acknowledging that, 'It's okay . . . it's just what brains do'. This advice may sound trite, but recent neuroscientific research examining brain activity associated with self-kindness suggests that doing such things can reduce or neutralise the brain's reaction to threat.

- ✔ When checking in with your body you might wish to ask yourself, 'How are my toes feeling now?' Pause to observe this feeling, then move up the body . . . 'How are my legs feeling now?' And so on, moving up the body. In some areas you may feel little or nothing. In others you may feel sensations such as tingling, stiffness, tension or heaviness. This part of the exercise is simply about checking in with the body in the here and now. It's about seeing things as they are in this moment — not changing them in any way.

- ✔ As thoughts come into your mind, recognise that you're having them, acknowledge them and then let them go. You may find it helpful to imagine the thoughts floating off on a cloud, drifting downriver, rolling away like the credits at the end of a film, or being put in a box to be dealt with later. Experiment and discover which approach works for you.

Grouping tasks

At the start of the day, try to plan how you will tackle work tasks. The tasks that you need to pay most attention to must be done when you're fresh and mentally alert, so do them first.

If you're feeling tired or sluggish, take a five-minute walk, if possible, or get a quick breath of fresh air. If it's late in the afternoon and you're feeling tired, ask yourself whether getting certain tasks done today is critical. Maybe they can wait until tomorrow morning when you're fresher.

Try to group your tasks into blocks of time, according to the different ways you use your brain to work on them. Remember, routine tasks involving little thought use less energy than tasks that involve decision-making or the creation of a new concept. Schedule time to do the latter when you're likely to be feeling fresh.

Starting the day by going through emails is a common mistake. Schedule emailing later on in the day in order to use your peak level of performance on the tasks that are most important.

Dealing with distractions

Avoiding everyday disruptions in the modern-day workplace can be challenging. Phones ring, emails and text messages ping, and people unexpectedly appear at your desk.

Switching between tasks reduces your productivity and can increase the pressure you're working under. Although many of us would say that these distractions are outside our control, in reality we can generally take steps to minimise them.

Ask yourself:

- Can I divert my phone for a short while today while I tackle the tasks that need most concentration?
- Can I switch off or silence my mobile phone for a while?
- Can I log off for a while so that incoming emails won't distract me?
- Can I ask people not to disturb me for a while?
- Can I find somewhere quiet to work where I won't be disturbed?
- Is being contactable 24/7 organisational culture, or am I just imposing this on myself?

Simple actions like logging off from your email account or silencing your phone can help you complete your most important work tasks more quickly. You'll be surprised at the results.

Mindfully Managing your Emotions

When you have lots to do, the calmer and more focused you remain, the better. As emotions are regulated by the primitive brain (refer to Chapter 1), remaining rational when in the grip of strong emotions is hard. Mindfulness can be used as a technique for working constructively with intense emotions such as fear and anger that often lead to misunderstandings and conflicts.

A simple mindfulness technique involves sitting with your eyes closed and focusing on your breathing. By concentrating on the rhythm of your breaths, you develop a sense of detachment, which stops your thoughts from spiralling further and further into depression or anxiety. In time you start to realise that thoughts come and go of their own accord, and that your conscious self is distinct from your thoughts. Refer to Chapter 3 for tips on how to practise mindfulness of breath.

How your body affects your mind

When seeking to manage your emotions, you need to recognise that whenever you encounter a situation, your thoughts trigger a physiological reaction in your body. Bodily tensions and sensations have more of an impact on your thoughts and behaviour than you might think. The model in Figure 4-1 can help you understand what's going on and stop yourself spiralling into over-thinking, anxiety and distraction.

When you understand the link between thoughts, emotions and the body (physiology), you can start to develop more helpful strategies for recognising and managing your emotions.

Mindfulness can help you to better manage your emotions in three important ways:

  ✔ **Mindfulness helps you to train your brain to treat thoughts as 'mental processes' rather than reality.** This change can stop you responding on auto-pilot, triggering a physiological reaction in your body and sending you spiralling further and further into the unwanted emotion.

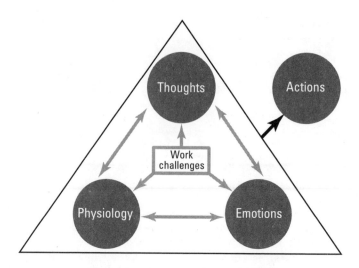

Figure 4-1: The interplay between thoughts, emotions and physiology.

✔ **Mindfulness helps you to live your life in the present moment.** It reduces your tendency to try to anticipate the future ('This could damage my reputation') or link to past experiences ('At my last company people were fired for less!'). Focusing on the present helps you to notice, manage and process emotions.

✔ **Mindfulness helps you to accept emotions.** Accept the fact that you're human, and from time to time you'll be sad, anxious or angry — being so is natural and part of being human. You need to acknowledge the emotion, but not dwell on it, or add further fuel to the fire. Mindfulness encourages self-compassion and acceptance — being kind to oneself. By accepting things as they are, right here, right now, you don't perpetuate unhelpful emotional reactions to circumstances.

Trying the 'Managing emotions mindfully' exercise

This exercise helps you slow down your mental chatter and reconnect with your body. When practised regularly, you'll be quicker at detecting emotions as they arise and able to take steps to stop them escalating if they're unhelpful.

Go to a quiet place for between 5 and 30 minutes (depending on how emotional you are and how much time you have!). Sit in a comfortable upright position with your feet firmly on the floor. Now follow these steps:

1. **Focus on air entering your lungs on the in-breath, and leaving your lungs on the out-breath.** Observe how your chest feels and how your skin feels as you breathe.

2. **Observe any emotions you are experiencing.** For example, anger, fear or worry. Just observe — don't try to fix them or make them go away.

3. **Acknowledge the noises that surround you.** Sounds in the room, sounds outside the room and sounds elsewhere in the building or outside. Possibly even sounds in your body. Use these sounds as an anchor for your attention. Again no need to fix them or make them go away — just notice they are there.

4. **Check how your body feels at this moment in time by carrying out a body scan.** Start at your toes. Can you feel any sensations or stiffness? Continue the exercise by slowly moving up your body. If you do detect tension or discomfort, pause for a short while, and try releasing the tension progressively as you breathe out. Continue your body scan, exploring any bodily tensions or sensations until you've scanned from the tip of your toes to the crown of your head.

5. **Observe your emotions again.** Kindly and gently direct your attention to your emotions. Notice how they are in the present moment. Are they the same as before or different? If so, what has changed? When you're ready, open your eyes.

Dealing with difficult people

In your home and social life, you usually get to choose the people you wish to spend time with. In a work situation, that's often not the case. You encounter both clients and colleagues who you may find difficult to deal with. Working with difficult people can trigger strong emotional reactions, which can take up a lot of your mental energy, robbing you of the mental resources you need to deal with your workload.

Mindfulness can help you to respond to these situations in a more resilient manner.

Asking 'What's really going on?'

The first thing to explore is what's really going on. Why do you find this person so difficult or challenging? You need to recognise what responses have been triggered within you when you encounter this person. What are your thoughts and emotions? What has changed in your body? Has your heart rate or breathing increased? Are you feeling tension or even pain?

By recognising your own emotional state and bodily tension, you will be better equipped to deal with the situation. When approaching encounters with difficult people mindfully, you can reduce the pain and suffering for all concerned, and find ways to work together more productively.

You can't always control the things that happen in your work day, but you can choose how you respond to them.

Understanding whose problem it is

The next thing to ask is 'Whose problem is it?'

Consider Bob, the account manager described earlier in the chapter. Bob's boss saw his potential and in his appraisal set him challenging goals in an effort to prepare him for a possible promotion. Bob didn't know his boss was preparing him for promotion. He thought that he had set him up to fail and that his appraisal goals were an attempt to get rid of him. As a result, he started to hate his boss.

What can you learn from this scenario? Bob's failure to clarify why his boss had set him the goals made him jump to the wrong conclusions. His reaction to, and behaviour towards, his boss was making the situation worse.

When dealing with a person you find difficult, take a few moments to think about whose problem it is. Is it your problem? Or is it the other person who has a problem with you?

Thoughts are not necessarily facts. Drawing conclusions based on thoughts rather than facts is all too easy.

Bob's colleague encourages him to take a more mindful approach in future. In preparation for meeting his boss, Bob took a few minutes to practise some mindfulness. When Bob next met his boss, he started with a clean slate. He admitted that he's finding the goals he was set challenging. His boss laughed and said, 'They're supposed to be challenging. I set them to help you get ready for your next promotion!'

By practising mindfulness, Bob discovered that his thoughts are not all facts, and decided to start afresh with his boss. He knew he'd be tense upon entering the meeting, so he practised a little mindfulness to put himself in a more open frame of mind.

Bear these tips in mind:

- ✔ When preparing for a difficult encounter, practise mindfulness. Doing so stops your thoughts churning and releases any tension you're holding.

- ✔ Start the encounter with an open mind, as if you're meeting the person for the first time.

- ✔ If you feel your body tensing up during the meeting, or you start to become emotional, congratulate yourself on recognising that fact, and try to let go of the tension.

- ✔ After the meeting, spend a few moments reflecting on what (if anything) was different about this encounter with the person.

The 'difficult' person may be creating the problem despite your best efforts to work productively with them. Treat this thought as a theory only; remember, this thought is not necessarily a fact. You can't easily change the other person's behaviour and attitude towards you, but you can choose your response and behaviour.

If, despite your best efforts, your working relationship doesn't improve, just accept that you find this person difficult to work with and commit to making a conscious effort not to make things any worse. Use mindfulness to help you recognise and release any physical tension. Become conscious of your own emotional state. Recognise when thoughts start to spiral, and bring yourself back to the present moment. Mentally reward yourself for being more aware of what's going on, and taking steps to make the best of it.

No magic bullet or cure-all exists. You're not a machine; you're human and as such you will from time to time experience unhelpful emotions that impact on your relationships. Living your whole life in a relaxed, emotionless manner is unnatural. But living in a constantly heightened state of arousal is unhealthy and unproductive. Practising mindfulness gradually trains your brain to come back to the present moment and see things as they really are. Then you can break out of life on auto-pilot and respond to life's challenges (such as difficult people) wisely.

Mindful Ways to Maintain Peak Performance

Some people think that practising mindfulness will subdue you or make you less ambitious and driven. This is a myth. Some of the most productive people on this planet practise mindfulness because it helps them maintain peak performance for longer periods.

Current thought on the psychology of performance suggests that in order to maintain peak performance you need to focus upon the factors that allow you to flourish and to achieve your aims. To do so, you need to practise mental skills to develop the power of your mind. Assuming that you're clear about your aims at work, you need to be mentally and physically fit to perform at your best. Don't worry; taking up marathon running won't be necessary! You just need to work out what 'peak performance' looks and feels like for you.

This simple 'Mindfulness for peak performance' exercise takes only moments, but can save you hours of time wasted through working in a distracted, pressured manner. You could do this in a few minutes, or extend it if you have more time.

1. **Settle yourself in a chair.** Sit in a comfortable upright, dignified position with your feet firmly on the floor and your arms resting comfortably. Focus on the physical sensations of taking a few breaths. Close your eyes or hold them in soft focus.

2. **Acknowledge what's going on in your mind (your thoughts) in a detached manner, rather like watching the closing credits of a film.**

3. **Observe how your body is feeling in this present moment.** Tune in to any areas where you know you tend to hold tension. (For example, your neck, shoulders, jaw or stomach.) Approach them and explore how they feel, like a scientist observing the subject of a research study. See whether you can release the tension and let it go. Don't beat yourself up if you can't.

4. **Ask yourself, 'At this moment, what do I need to do to return to peak performance?' Listen for a response.** Maybe you need to actively release the tension from your body, take a quick walk (even if just to the coffee machine) or work on something different for a while.

Use this technique to check in with yourself on a regular basis. When practised regularly, you'll quickly recognise the physical and mental signs telling you you've slipped from peak performance.

 An excellent way to improve your working life is to consciously make an effort to live more in the present moment. By being in the moment you make better decisions, see things more clearly and become more creative. You can enjoy precious everyday moments with your loved ones, and gain nourishment from the simplest of everyday things.

Being Kind to Yourself

The author Henry James said: 'Three things in human life are important. The first is to be kind. The second is to be kind. And the third is to be kind.'

Authentic leadership, resonant leadership and mindful leadership are new forms of leadership theory. They all emphasise the need to be kind to yourself, and with good reason. Research shows that people who make a conscious effort to be kind to themselves demonstrate greater well-being than those who judge themselves.

When something goes wrong, or you make a mistake, you may be far too quick to point the finger of blame at yourself. As humans we tend to beat ourselves up for all failures, large or small, reducing our self-belief and self-esteem. You may unconsciously poison yourself with toxic self-criticism. In an attempt to anticipate the future, you may make up your own stories and then react to them as if they were reality. Doing so can lead you into a spiral of depression or anxiety.

By being kind to yourself, you can increase your personal resilience to the pressures of life by stopping your brain from jumping to conclusions and spiralling into stress and panic. In turn, you'll increase your happiness and productivity.

If you, like many other people, struggle with self-kindness, try this 'Cultivating kindness' exercise. You may find it challenging at first, but it gets easier with practice. Follow these steps:

- ✔ **Settle yourself into a comfortable, upright, dignified position, and focus your attention on your breathing for a minute or so.**

- ✔ **Send yourself some kindness.** Imagine giving yourself a hug and accepting yourself exactly as you are — perfect in your human imperfection. Picture yourself surrounded by a warm glow of kindness.

- ✔ **Send some kindness to a dear friend.** Thank them for their friendship and support. Wish them well and imagine them surrounded by a warm glow of kindness.

- ✔ **Send some kindness to a neutral person — someone you've never met.** Wish them a happy life and send them kind thoughts. Imagine them surrounded by a warm glow of kindness.

- ✔ **Send some kindness to a hostile person — someone who you may have argued with or who makes you feel uncomfortable.** Wish them a happy life and send them kind thoughts. Imagine them surrounded by a warm glow of kindness.

Discovering the neuroscience of kindness and compassion

Fear can trigger a threat response in your brain. Your reaction is often disproportionate to the actual provocation. When in the grip of this strong emotion, your capacity for higher 'rational brain' thinking is diminished, and you're likely to revert to rote behaviours stored in the more primitive areas of your brain.

When you're kind to yourself, and accept yourself as human, prone to making mistakes from time to time, but doing your best, you're far less likely to trigger your threat system unnecessarily. Self-kindness can help you to enjoy life more, improve your relationships, increase your self-esteem and make you feel happier. All these things are likely to contribute to improved performance at work.

Try this 'Experiencing self-kindness' exercise. When you're upset, give yourself a hug, place your hand on your heart or gently rock your body. Your body responds to the physical warmth and care (just imagining a hug works in a similar way too). Hugging yourself has soothing benefits. Research indicates that physical touch releases oxytocin in your brain — the hormone associated with love and bonding. Oxytocin provides a sense of security, soothes distressing emotions and calms cardiovascular stress.

Rewiring your brain

The more you repeat a thought or activity, the more you strengthen the neural pathway associated with that specific thought or activity in your brain. The stronger the neural connection, the easier it is to repeat. Many thoughts and activities, when repeated often enough, become stored in the more primitive areas of your brain as 'habits' — things you do without thinking. Opinion is divided about how long it takes to form a habit. Estimates range from an average of 21 to 64 days.

By consciously making an effort to catch yourself when you're being overly self-critical, and accepting things as they are, over time you can rewire your brain to become more kind to yourself. Mindfulness exercises always include elements of self-kindness.

The cultivation of self-kindness is something that many people struggle with, finding it easier to be kind to someone else than themselves. Self-kindness and acceptance are important elements of mindfulness. By learning to accept yourself, faults and all, an enormous, self-imposed burden is lifted and life becomes easier. Practising self-kindness significantly increases your resilience at work.

Last, but by no means least . . .

It goes without saying that the healthier and happier you are the more resilient you will be. Be kind to yourself! Eat well, drink enough water and don't forget to get some exercise.

Stop for lunch and spend a few moments in the present moment, fully appreciating the act of eating — the flavour, the texture, the taste — and how it feels to eat.

If you can, when you go to work, park a little further away to get a short walk each day. Take the stairs not the lift. At the very least get up and stretch at your desk every hour.

Your body will thank you for it, and your boss should appreciate the positive impact of your improved resilience.

Chapter 5

Practising Mindfulness in the Digital Age

• •

In This Chapter

▶ Making technology work for you rather than control you

▶ Using technology mindfully to enhance communication

▶ Focusing with helpful techniques

• •

*T*his chapter helps you to manage one of the most beneficial but also most challenging aspects of living in the information age — digital technology. Mindfulness offers you the presence of mind to be able to choose when to use technology, to identify what sort of technology you need and to recognise when a more real-world approach is called for. When you do use technology, you discover how mindfulness offers a way of working with it that involves a greater degree of presence, wisdom and compassion.

Choosing When to Use Technology

Technology includes any application of scientific knowledge for practical purposes. In the industrial age, technology was dominated by mechanical machinery driven by the steam engine. But in the 21st Century, your daily life is probably dominated by digital technology. The explosion in the use of digital technology is impacting every single organisation in some way.

The evolution of the human brain didn't take modern technology into account. So these changes are creating a big challenge, even for the powerhouse that resides in your skull. The pervasive use of technology often means that you may not even question your use of email or texting to communicate — mindfulness offers a chance to momentarily reflect before you immerse yourself in sending another deluge of messages out into the World Wide Web.

Recognising the pros and cons of technology

Digital technology certainly has many benefits in the workplace. Communication via texts and instant messaging is almost immediate. Video conferencing means that time isn't wasted on travelling to meetings. Work can be completed on the move. With laptops and smartphones, you can stay connected and keep working on planes, trains and in automobiles. And with the processing power of computers, technology is used to manage huge amounts of data from customers to help you decide how best to serve their needs.

Are there any drawbacks to the use of technology? We think so, especially if you use it unskilfully. Here are a few disadvantages that are often overlooked:

- ✔ **Compulsive use of digital communication:** Email can change from a tool to an addiction. Constant checking of email, even when other tasks are more pressing, wastes both time and energy, and ultimately reduces the company's productivity.

- ✔ **Reduced ability to focus:** Too much use of technology can make you distracted, as you jump from one task to the next. A lack of extended time working on just one task reduces your brain's ability to focus.

- ✔ **Less face-to-face time:** The more time you spend using technology, the less time is available for face-to-face meetings. This reduction in human contact can make working relationships a little shallower and result in lower levels of trust and understanding between people.

- ✔ **Inefficiency resulting from multi-tasking:** With technology comes the temptation to multi-task. Multi-tasking leads to reduced productivity and a lack of satisfaction.

Mindfulness can help you to notice your new relationship with technology so that you're more in control rather than being a slave to your digital devices.

Rebalancing your use of technology

Using technology too much is a problem. If you're used to checking your phone every minute of the day for messages, you may struggle to concentrate when in a meeting or listening to your boss. Inefficient habits when online may mean that you end up surfing from one website to another instead of completing your tasks. And deciding to always communicate via technology rather than meeting face to face can lead to loss of opportunities to discuss new ideas and create a deeper and more trusting relationship with colleagues or customers.

Having described the downside to over-use of digital devices in the preceding section, you need to recognise that an aversion to technology can be an issue too. If you're the CEO of the organisation and decide not to make best use of technology, your competitors may surpass you. Using outdated technology may frustrate your staff and mean that you struggle to attract the talent you need to succeed.

A balanced approach is the answer. Most companies have embraced the use of technology, and that's probably a good thing. But you may not know how to use technology in a more mindful way so that you're not in a constant state of distraction or miscommunicating with others as you respond on a purely emotional level. We think that a set of strategies is required in the workplace to help individuals make more conscious choices in their use of technology.

One of the most effective ways of managing your technology is having downtime — time when you switch off from technology. Computers are different from humans. Computers work best if they're never switched off. They can go on and on working without rest. However, if you stay connected and switched on without time to recharge, you burn out. Your attentional resources deplete rapidly, as do your energy levels, enthusiasm and intelligence. So having a few minutes, a few hours, a few days and sometimes a few weeks away from technology is key to your success.

Here are a few ways to create digital downtime, based on how much time you have available:

- ✔ **A few minutes:** Take a few minutes break every half hour or so if you work on a computer all day. Taking a step back, concentrating on a few deep, conscious breaths and walking around are good for your body and mind.

- ✔ **A few hours:** When the work day is over, take a break from the screen. It's very common for people to work on a screen all day, and relax at home by watching another screen. Refresh yourself by socialising, doing a spot of mindfulness practice, taking up a hobby or participating in sport.

- ✔ **A few days:** Take time off from technology every week. Aim for at least one day off per week if possible. Saturday is a good day for many people. See whether you can leave your phone behind, avoid checking email or social media, and do something more natural and energising.

- ✔ **A few weeks**: If you can, take a few weeks' holiday at least once a year. On holiday, see if you can have an extended period of time away from phones, computers and so on. This is probably when you'll have your creative juices flowing as your mind comes up with unique solutions for challenges you've been facing in the workplace or at home. We've had some of our greatest business ideas whilst on a mindfulness retreat, which involved mainly sitting, walking, stretching and with no access to phones, TVs or iPads. If you're connected digitally every day, you'll be amazed at how clear your mind becomes following a break from all that for a week or so.

Communicating Mindfully

Communication lies at the heart of being human. In the workplace, you're bound to be communicating often with others. And when you're not communicating with others, you're communicating with yourself, being aware of your thoughts, emotions and even sensations in your body.

Mindful communication is about bringing a greater level of conscious awareness and reflection to how you communicate. With greater awareness, you're better able to understand what others wish to express to you, as well as able to choose when and how to communicate your own thoughts.

Communication has been transformed by technology. Whereas in the past face-to-face conversations were the only way to communicate, you can now share your thoughts in lots of different ways. With the advent of the telephone, a person on the other side of the world was only a few button pushes away. And with the creation of the internet came not only email but also live video chat via platforms such as Skype and Google Hangouts — and free to boot! Finally, communication took another step change with the creation of social media, dominated by Facebook, Twitter and LinkedIn.

For example, just today we've been on social media to share a blog post, exchanged several emails about a meeting tomorrow, had two phone calls from colleagues about work on a website, and exchanged three text messages and some WhatsApp messages. And this is a very typical day, where we kept our phones off for large chunks of the day whilst working on this book! If we didn't know about that discipline of switching off technology, we would be getting disturbed all day.

Face-to-face conversations are now just one option and are often the less-favoured option because of the investment of time required. Are face-to-face meetings worth the effort? Regular face-to-face interactions build up social networks in the brain through subtle visual cues and signals. If you spend thousands of hours online, you miss out on this training. Young people growing up in the modern age may have a reduced ability to socialise resulting from lack of face-to-face time.

Face-to-face communication has many inherent benefits that aren't so easy to access online or over the phone. These benefits include:

- ✔ **The personal touch:** When you've met a colleague, customer or supplier in person, the relationship changes. You're more likely to keep in touch and you have a clear image associated with that name. The in-person meeting can lead to conversations, ideas and insights that would never be discussed in other ways.

- ✔ **Non-verbal communication:** Spending time face to face means that you pick up all sorts of clues from a person's body language that you won't get via other forms of communication. This point is key. A pause when you mention the new deal may tell you that the other person is somewhat reluctant to commit to it. If you manage a salesperson via email alone, you never pick up that they speak too loudly and quickly. You don't understand the pressure your designer is under until you see their face. With this extra information, you can make better decisions.

✔ **Teams work better when together:** Research described in the *Journal of Computer-Mediated Communication* found that teams working face to face made fewer errors and reported improved teamwork and performance.

✔ **Dealing with tricky situations:** When a situation is slightly emotionally charged, a face-to-face conversation can work best. Positive non-verbal communication can help to diffuse unnecessary tension. Online communication may cause the difficulties to spiral into bigger problems if not nipped in the bud.

A mindful communicator chooses what is the most effective form of communication and then gives that communication their full attention. Mindful communication also keeps in mind the limits of the medium of communication.

Here are seven forms of communication, rated hierarchically according to the level of feedback they provide — least to most:

1. **Instant messaging:** Expect instant replies. Little or no emotion. Fast.

2. **Text:** Very short; great for catching attention but too short for any meaningful communication. No emotional communication to couch the words spoken. The same message can potentially be read as positive or negative.

3. **Email:** Lacks any emotional feedback. Neutral emails can be read as negative or rude.

4. **Social media:** Some forms also include emotional feedback, but the stream of messages often scatters the attention thinly. Not often used in a business environment, but this trend is changing.

5. **Telephone:** Tone of voice can provide much more feedback than preceding methods. Needs to be used more, not less.

6. **Video chat:** Probably the best form of technology-based communication. Facial expression enhances the information exchanged. Some of the social network parts of your brain are receiving feedback and engaging.

7. **Face-to-face meeting:** The ultimate form of communication. Tone of voice, body posture, speed of speech and a wide range of facial expressions are

clearly observable. No risk of technology breakdown. A handshake or friendly hug, together with eye contact, increase trust and improve wellbeing. Slow.

Emailing mindfully

Email is both incredibly convenient and incredibly stressful. As the existence of more than 3 billion email accounts demonstrates, however, it is certainly popular.

Email is a tool for your own use. If you check email when you need to, and respond efficiently, all may be well. But you may be in the habit of checking email too often, hoping for that next interesting message to come flying through.

Mindful emailing is using email with greater awareness and wisdom. The purpose of using email is to communicate for the benefit of both you and your recipient.

Try these tips to help you use email more mindfully and productively:

- ✔ **Make a brief emailing plan:** Use a notebook to jot down who you plan to send emails to and a few brief points that you want to make each day. Then, write those emails first. You can check new emails later. Making a plan may only take a couple of minutes but can save you hours of time reading and replying to emails that aren't important.

- ✔ **Watch out for email addiction:** Decide in advance how many times a day you're going to check your emails. For some people, once is enough; for others, once an hour is necessary. Unless your primary role is dealing with emails, you need to ensure that you're not in the habit of constantly checking your inbox. If you find that even sticking to a nominal number of checks a day isn't working, write down the actual times of day that you're going to open your inbox. Imposing discipline on yourself in this way helps you retrain your mind so that you focus on what's in front of you rather than being constantly distracted by often unnecessary messages.

- ✔ **Breathe before sending:** Before you send an email, take three mindful breaths. Doing so helps you to become more mindful, gives you an opportunity to reflect on what you've written and helps you to stay focused.

✔ **See your email from the other person's perspective:** After you've taken your mindful breaths (refer to preceding point), imagine how the other person is going to feel when they read your email. You may decide that it needs editing before you send it. You may even give them a call instead!

✔ **Send at least one positive email every day:** Focusing on the good helps to rebalance your brain's natural negativity bias and makes both you and your recipient feel better. Praise an employee for settling into the team so quickly, thank your boss for their help with the report yesterday or congratulate Michelle on her sales presentation. A positive email is a great way to start the day.

✔ **Control your emails; don't let them control you:** Choose who you want to respond to instead of reacting to every new email that lands in your inbox. Cultivate good email habits, such as limiting the time you spend on them and focusing only on those that are essential.

Be mindful and present as you deal with emails. Use your favourite mindful exercises before and after emailing to help you achieve greater focus.

Turn off your message notifications, so that you aren't alerted each time a new one arrives. Doing so is your first step towards reducing the amount of time you waste in this way.

Phoning mindfully

One day one of our clients wanted to do something different. When he received a routine email from accounts, he decided to phone the sender rather than simply email his response. The phone seemed to ring for quite some time before a tentative voice said, 'Hello?' Our client told the woman that he was the person she'd been emailing for years but had never actually spoken to. They went on to have a pleasant conversation and the person in accounts said the call made her feel less like a machine and more like someone who actually works with other people. That encounter was certainly a wake-up call for our client!

Mindful phoning means bringing a greater degree of awareness to the process of being on the phone. With mindful phoning, you need to be aware of several things:

✔ What the other person is saying

✔ Their tone of voice

✔ What you want to say

✔ Your state of mind

✔ What you want to achieve from the conversation

✔ How you can be of help to the other person

Try this exercise next time you make a phone call:

1. **Take a few moments to be mindful:** Practise a short mindful pause by feeling your breathing, your bodily sensations or connecting with one of your senses.

2. **Write down the aims of the conversation you're about to have:** This only takes a few seconds.

3. **Stand up:** If you usually sit down all day facing a computer, making a phone call provides a great opportunity to get to your feet and move your body around a bit.

4. **Listen more than you speak:** Make sure that you listen to the other person's tone of voice as well as their actual words.

5. **Be aware of your emotions:** If the conversation makes you feel anxious or angry, notice the feeling in your body. Feel the emotion with your breathing and then speak from your wise mind rather than reacting automatically to your feelings, saying things you may later regret. Try to tap into greater levels of mindfulness as the conversation progresses. Breathing mindfully can help.

6. **End the conversation when you need to, rather than dragging it out unnecessarily.**

The key to mindful phoning is to do a short mindful exercise before phoning. Then you'll be more focused and present during the call itself.

Using a smartphone mindfully

Smartphones are pretty smart. With them you can check emails, update social media, surf the internet, take photos and make videos, edit videos, upload to YouTube, write a blog post, access loads of apps, work with documents, enable video chat, manage your calendar, find a restaurant, use global maps with GPS, find out the time anywhere on the planet, read and listen to books, buy products, and even learn mindfulness! Oh, we almost forgot: You can make phone calls with them too.

Smartphones are particularly addictive and can drain your mental focus and creativity when used excessively. Compulsively checking your smartphone becomes a problem when it starts interfering with your everyday life. Reading your emails instead of listening to someone speaking in a meeting is one example. But what about scanning through your Facebook updates when you're listening to a customer on the phone — such behaviour may cost you and your company lost revenue.

If you think that you need an injection of mindfulness to bring your smartphone habits under control, give these actions a go:

- ✔ **Be conscious:** When you feel the desire to check your emails or suddenly find yourself gazing at your beloved iPhone, ask yourself what emotion you're feeling. What emotion are you trying to avoid? Anxiety, boredom, loneliness perhaps?

- ✔ **Be disciplined:** Turn off your device in certain situations, such as when you're driving, attending meetings, playing with your children and eating supper with your partner — all the key moments in your day when focus is called for.

- ✔ **Ride the wave:** When you feel an urge to check your phone, take mindful breaths and be with the feeling rather than acting on it. Your compulsion should gradually weaken.

- ✔ **Don't give up:** If you relapse into your 24/7 phone-checking habit, don't feel defeated. Try again. You don't need to beat yourself up about it. Your smartphone really is addictive, so be friendly to yourself and have another go.

If you can afford to do so, use one phone for work and another for your personal life. That way you can literally switch off from work at the end of the day.

Here are a few strategies to help you manage your smartphone with mindfulness:

- ✔ Don't check your messages in the morning or evening.

- ✔ Switch off notifications on your phone except those for text messages.

✔ Set your phone on flight mode whenever you're focusing on a piece of work.

✔ Turn off your phone when attending meetings, going for a walk or enjoying time with friends.

Engaging with social media mindfully

Social media, such as Facebook, Twitter and LinkedIn, has changed the way many businesses operate. Entire companies have emerged to help organisations manage their social media — the way they connect with their customers and suppliers. And traditional advertising is finding itself working less effectively as social media is far more interactive, engaging and fun for consumers.

Here are some key principles to consider when using social media in a way that means personal and business use overlap, as often happens in small to medium-sized organisations:

✔ **See business social media as part of your working day:** So, when you're with family, keep it off. Just as it would be rude to start checking your emails when your partner is talking to you, so too is using social media for business purposes.

✔ **Update at set times:** Update social media using apps such as Buffer or HootSuite so that you reduce the time you spend turning on and off all the separate social media channels.

✔ **Be friendly:** You can easily end up seeing people as just another number. They're not — behind each connection is a human being. If they have a comment or question, do respond. If you have too many messages to respond to individually, acknowledge their comments in a group response.

✔ **Seek to make genuine connections rather than superficial contacts:** Customers will feel better for it, and so will you. And those connections may lead to more business.

✔ **Give more than you receive:** Seek to help others. If someone has a question that isn't directly related to your business, you can still help out. Just as you wouldn't ignore someone in person who asked you a question, don't ignore them when online either.

Writing mindfully

Pretty much every modern business in the world has a presence on the internet. And websites need content. Although such content is increasingly in the form of video and audio, the internet is still awash with the written word. To be successful online, you need to be able to write well or hire someone with that skill.

Writing effectively is also important for communication. Emails, text messages, reports and even presentations involve writing. So, how can you write in a way that engages your readers? And what does mindfulness have to contribute to the art of writing?

Having written five books, Shamash has spent a lot of time over the past few years just writing. And here's what he learnt about writing in a mindful way:

- ✔ **You need to look after yourself:** Writing well requires that your brain is working at its optimal level. You can't achieve this state for long if you're feeling tired, hungry, cold or stressed out. Ensure that you go to bed on time and get enough sleep. Eat something every few hours, and make sure that meals contain plenty of fruit and vegetables. Keep a bottle of water to hand — the brain works much better when properly hydrated. Make sure that the room is at a comfortable temperature; you'll feel more relaxed as a result. Finally, if you're under a lot of pressure take regular breaks and find time to socialise and exercise. Even if you're facing a big deadline, try to prioritise breaks and make time for mindfulness practice. Doing so will make you more efficient.

- ✔ **Timing is everything:** Keep a time journal to identify at what time of day you're most efficient. Then do your writing at that time. You need to make that time sacred — avoid phone calls, meetings, emails and any other distractions.

- ✔ **Mindfulness exercises keep you focused:** Practise mindfulness exercises as often as you can. Use the mindful body scan (refer to Chapter 3) or do some informal mindfulness when you're walking or eating. Try to connect with your senses whenever mindfulness comes to mind.

- ✔ **Outside distractions need to be removed:** To be able to write well, you need to focus. Block out as many distractions as you can. Silence your phone; don't tell other people where you're working; close all other programs on your computer.

✔ **You need to manage your inner critic:** You need to take that inner voice who judges everything you do in hand. For some reason, the process of writing really wakes it up! Fortunately, you can use mindfulness to manage your inner critic. First, you notice those negative thoughts and then you say to yourself 'inner critic' and have a little smile. Smiling sends a signal to your brain (neurons connect the brain to the muscles that are used to smile) that you're not scared of that voice. Fighting or frantically running away from your inner critic can exacerbate its judgemental voice. Each time you address your inner critic in this way, you weaken its power until eventually, if you're lucky, it dies altogether.

✔ **Writing non-judgementally is a powerful tool:** Mindfulness means moment-to-moment non-judgemental awareness. So, try a period of time just writing down whatever comes into your head, without judging it. Don't correct sentences, delete words or fix spellings. Just go with the flow and write. Doing so is a true mindfulness process — being in the moment and allowing whatever arises to be as it is. Later on, you can go back and correct your mistakes.

If you write on a computer, lots of software is available to help you stay focused. Shamash likes to simply put Microsoft Word into 'Focus' mode. Then you just see the document you're writing and all other windows disappear — ideal for you budding mindful writers out there! Another option is Ommwriter — available for Mac, PC and iPad.

Chapter 6

Using Mindfulness to Assist Different Business Functions

• •

• •

Cultivating mindfulness is a valuable skill for staff working at all levels of the organisation, in all business functions, in all industries. Mindfulness won't diminish your drive for excellence and attention to what's important. It won't make you weak or ineffective, or brainwash you into donating all your worldly goods to a worthwhile cause in a far-flung corner of the world. Also, despite media portrayal of mindfulness, you don't have to sit cross-legged on a cushion, light incense or become religious!

To get the most from mindfulness, you really need to attend a course, and practise mindfulness each day, but the hints and tips in this chapter should prove valuable to specific business functions. Many of the tips and techniques provided are equally applicable to multiple job roles. We make a start by looking at human resources.

Mindfulness for Human Resources

What's in a name? 'HR' (human resources), 'personnel' or even 'human capital management' are all names for the business function responsible for recruitment and selection of staff, defining job roles and setting pay structures. HR teams may also develop policies on how staff should behave and be treated, including equal opportunities and employee assistance programmes. Where the learning and development function sits under HR, the department is also responsible for developing staff at all levels. Although some aspects of HR, such as telling someone they've got the job or have been promoted, are satisfying, other parts can be highly stressful. Potentially stressful parts of the job include dealing with grievances and dismissals. In this section are suggestions on how mindfulness can help you to mindfully manage three key functions of most HR departments.

Managing downsizing and redundancies mindfully

The economic downturn led to cost-cutting initiatives in both the public and private sectors. In many organisations, these initiatives resulted in downsizing and redundancies, year on year.

While you may not be able to halt the tide of redundancies, you can undertake the process in a manner that's kinder to yourself and those people at risk of redundancy. We start by focusing on the impact that managing redundancies has on you.

Although managing redundancies and dismissals is likely to be a key element of your work that you've probably studied and practised over the years, this doesn't necessarily make it any easier. Even the most cold hearted of HR professionals are likely to experience some form of negative response to the task. As Chapter 4 explains, everything that you do or think has an impact on your thoughts, emotions and physiology, but in most cases you're unaware of the impact. This lack of awareness can be a good thing because it frees up your brain to work on other things. It can also be bad news if you start to unwittingly activate your sympathetic nervous system, flooding your body with powerful hormones that can be damaging. You may also unwittingly carry around tension in your body, which can have a profound impact on your decision-making. So although you may think that you're giving your best at all times, your actions and responses may be being governed by a host of things you're completely unaware of.

This is where mindfulness comes in. Mindfulness training progressively trains you to direct your full attention to where you want it to be. It allows you to passively observe the interplay between your thoughts, emotions and physiology, and make conscious choices about how to best respond, rather than being governed by your unconscious mental programming.

Another factor to consider is the potential impact of mirror neurons. *Mirror neurons* may cause you to experience the emotions of the people surrounding you, which may impact on your decisions and behaviour. Mindfulness helps you to focus attention on the present-moment experience, allowing you to notice when your emotions are being influenced by mirror neurons, and decide on a wise course of action.

While you can't necessarily 'manage' the emotions of others, you can take steps to avoid any negative emotions you are harbouring from spiralling out of control. By being fully present in meetings with others, you can observe as and when emotions start to spiral and take steps to avoid things escalating.

Here are a few mindful ways in which you can keep your meetings on track when strong emotions arise in others:

- ✔ **Take a few moments out.** Change the course of the conversation or just pause for a few moments to avoid adding more fuel to the fire.

- ✔ **Acknowledge the emotions, and try to help the person identify the thoughts driving them.** You can ask them, for example, 'I can see you're really upset. Would you like to share with me what's going through your mind?'

- ✔ **Demonstrate empathy.** Although you've a job to do, the world may be falling apart for the employee in front of you. Be as kind and compassionate as you can be while still ensuring that you deliver the organisational messages you need to.

- ✔ **Cultivate empathy.** If you find yourself suffering from compassion fatigue (common in the caring professions) and becoming immune to the suffering of others, make it a personal priority to cultivate empathy. Mindfulness can help you do so. You need to care about the people you are dealing with professionally while at the same time ensuring that you do the right thing for your organisation.

You may also wish to try out some of the mindfulness exercises described in this chapter.

Dealing with discipline and grievances mindfully

As with redundancies, dealing with discipline and grievances involves both care and doing the right thing (legally and ethically) for your organisation.

Preparing well for this sort of meeting is crucial. Most HR people are fully aware of the need to check the facts from all concerned, company policy and the law. What you may fail to do is check that you're mentally prepared for the meeting. In other words, you need to ensure that you enter the meeting in the present moment rather than your body being there but your attention continually being hijacked by thoughts about other jobs you have to do or what you'll be doing when you get home. You also need to try to ensure that your thinking isn't overly influenced by past experiences or by what people *may* be saying or how they *may* be behaving.

Only through practising mindfulness regularly do you gain an appreciation of the elaborate stories that your brain creates when trying to anticipate the future. The problem with these stories is that your brain can treat them as reality, and you can start to experience emotions in response. For example, if when entering a grievance session you think that the manager concerned will become angry and the employee tearful, you may unconsciously interact with the manager in an assertive or even aggressive manner and treat the employee with patience and concern.

By being in the present moment and following an appropriate meeting structure, allowing each part to unfold moment by moment and responding to present-moment facts, your meeting is likely to run more smoothly for all concerned.

Increasing employee engagement

Several research studies suggest that training staff in mindfulness can increase employee engagement. In addition, mindfulness has been shown to improve interpersonal relations, help employees improve the quality of relationships, increase resilience and improve task performance and decision-making. Mindfulness training can improve your ability to cope effectively with your own and other's daily stresses, thus improving the quality of your relationships.

Applying some techniques

The following techniques have been developed for HR staff, but may be equally applicable and useful for other business functions.

Dropping into the present moment

When dealing with difficult issues, maintaining your balance and wellbeing by dropping into the present moment every now and then is important. Doing so helps you to:

- ✔ Observe what's grabbing your attention and regain control when your thoughts are spiralling.

- ✔ Release any tension you're experiencing and reduce the risk of your physiological responses impacting on your decisions.

- ✔ Shift yourself from avoidance mode to an approach mode state of mind (refer to Chapter 1), which helps you to become more productive.

This can take as little as three minutes or be extended to take up to ten minutes.

Sit yourself in a comfortable upright position. Close your eyes or hold them in soft focus. Regain your equilibrium using this *NOW* technique:

1. **Notice (but don't judge or start to interact with):**

   - The sounds in the room and nearby

   - How your body is feeling — any tensions or sensations

   - Any emotions you may be feeling

2. **Observe the impact (if any) that the points under 'Notice' above are having on one another.** For example, does a certain sound make your body tense? Are your emotions having any impact on your thoughts? Is a trend or theme emerging as you observe your thoughts? Again, you don't need to do anything or solve anything; just observe what's happening in the present moment.

3. **Wait.** Resist the temptation to jump into action based on what you've noticed and observed. Just let everything go and give your brain a break by focusing on nothing but your breath for a short while. Fully experience the present sensation as the breath enters

your body and leaves your body; do so playfully, as if for the first time.

Open your eyes and make a decision on what's the best use of your time *now*, in this moment.

Mindfully managing difficult meetings

When planning difficult meetings, such as discussing job losses or giving notice of redundancies, being in the present moment is important so that you can judge the situation as it unfolds based on present-moment facts rather than mental projections about what may happen in the future or did happen in the past.

Following these steps will help make the meeting less stressful for all concerned:

1. **Ensure that you have all the relevant documents ready and are fully acquainted with all the facts and people involved.** Be as well prepared as you possibly can be.

2. **Practise mindfulness for a short period.** Try the three-step focus break (refer to Chapter 4) or a mindful pause (refer to Chapter 3).

3. **Start the meeting by stating its purpose and what you are going to cover and specify when people will have the opportunity for questions.** This last point may sound obvious, but it's amazing how often this detail is missed when emotions are running high.

4. **Check in with yourself regularly to check that you are operating in approach mode in the present moment.** Periodically observe your thoughts or tune in to how a specific area of your body feels.

5. **Try to see things through the eyes of your audience.** They're likely to be feeling threatened, which will influence their thoughts and behaviour. When in the grip of strong emotions, they're unlikely to be fully aware of their words and actions. This situation is natural; try not to take people's responses personally. Try to remain kind and considerate, bearing in mind the situation these people find themselves in. Remember, while managing meetings like this may be a regular occurrence for you, being threatened with redundancy may be new to them.

6. **Be kind to yourself!** Meetings about redundancies or grievances, for example, can be unpleasant and emotions can run high. You are a human being and not a machine,

and as such you're entitled to feel emotional (angry, sad or even anxious). The important thing to remember is that the emotion is transient — it will come and go — and it won't last forever.

Mindfully supporting staff

In your role you're likely to have many one-to-one informal and formal meetings with staff who may be worried about a variety of work-related issues. Your role isn't only to provide them with sources of information and support, but also to tap into how you can best help them in this specific moment in time. Unfortunately, if you've been involved in many meetings with staff over the years, acting on auto-pilot is all too easy. You need to remember that each meeting is unique and should be approached with a beginner's mind — as if you're experiencing it for the first time. Although approaching meetings this way may require a little more effort, the outcomes make it worthwhile. Follow these steps:

- ✔ **Jump into the present moment by setting aside thoughts of what you were doing before the person walked in or what you need to do later on.** If you have time before the person arrives, practise a short mindfulness technique.

- ✔ **Closely observe what's unfolding in the present moment.** Rather than responding in a routine manner to what you think the person's needs are at this stage of the process, really listen to what is being said and how it's being said.

- ✔ **Respond based on what's being asked for in the present moment rather than on what you think you should be hearing.** Be honest, open and authentic.

- ✔ **Recap and summarise at key points in the meeting to clarify understanding and reassure the other person that you've heard and understood what they're saying.** A quick overview gives the other person the chance to correct your understanding if necessary.

- ✔ **Provide a quick summary at the end of the meeting and agree on what should happen next.**

- ✔ **Check in with yourself.** After the other person has left, let go of any tension or negative emotions you may be harbouring so that you're ready to tackle the next part of your day. A three-step body check (check out Chapter 3 for more) or three-step focus break (refer to Chapter 4) should help you do this.

Mindfulness for Occupational Health

A great deal of research has concluded that mindfulness is great for wellbeing. Hundreds of research studies over the past 40 years have demonstrated the effectiveness of mindfulness in reducing anxiety, stress and depression. Mindfulness has also been proven to help people with chronic pain, such as back pain, and even to boost immunity. Several workplace studies have demonstrated its effectiveness in reducing sickness absence from work.

Improving staff wellbeing with mindfulness

Taking proactive steps to improve staff wellbeing is now more important than ever. Ongoing restructures and redundancies are taking their toll on those who are lucky enough to still have a job. Research conducted in 1997 identified that, not only do survivors of redundancy frequently feel guilty, but continued uncertainty can have a huge impact on people's health and increase long-term sickness absence. A constant sense of uncertainty can cause excessive stress, which can also lead to increased occupational accidents and serious illness such as heart disease, high blood pressure or diabetes.

Organisations can work to improve the wellbeing of their staff in many ways. Offering mindfulness courses to staff is a good way to improve not only wellbeing but also productivity and interpersonal skills. Some organisations offer staff mindfulness courses in work time and some outside working hours; some make attendance on mindfulness courses compulsory for certain staff, while others prefer it to be optional. Some organisations prefer to stick to the most widely researched methods of teaching mindfulness, while others integrate aspects of mindfulness training with other wellbeing initiatives. See Chapter 8 for more information on introducing mindfulness to your organisation.

Tackling stress with mindfulness

It should come as no surprise that stress has become one of the greatest causes of long-term sickness absence from work. Mindfulness has been used to treat stress since the 1970s.

As with all mindfulness at work interventions, evaluating staff both before and after taking part in a mindfulness course using well-recognised measures is important. If you wish to reduce stress specifically, you first need to measure individuals' current levels of stress. Consider getting staff to complete the DASS 21 — a shortened version of the DASS (Depression Anxiety Stress Scales), developed by the University of New South Wales in Australia. The DASS 21 measures the severity of a range of symptoms common to depression, anxiety and stress. This measure can then be used as a benchmark pre- and post-mindfulness training.

Mindfulness isn't a silver bullet. Simply attending a mindfulness course will not reduce stress. Reducing stress takes effort and commitment on the part of the stressed participant, who needs to practise what they're taught for a short time every day for the entire duration of the eight-week course. Research suggests a direct correlation exists between time spent practising mindfulness and the benefits experienced. In general, the more time spent practising, the more benefit is derived. Note also that, if a staff member is *very severely* stressed, a mindfulness course may prove unsuitable as the staff member may not be in a fit state of mind to work with the techniques they're taught. In this instance, seeking clinical help would be wise.

Reducing sickness absence with mindfulness

Well people who are well managed result in a well organisation. Wellbeing at work isn't the sole responsibility of the occupational health team but the responsibility of the whole organisation. Policies and working practices can have a huge impact on staff wellbeing, and are worth reviewing if staff absence and sickness are on the increase.

Mindfulness can equip staff with the tools to deal with life's challenges more effectively, which can reduce stress and anxiety. Mindfulness can also help people to stop small things escalating out of control and causing unnecessary stress. Mindfulness can help people live with long-term health conditions, including back problems and even cancer, by giving them new ways of dealing with their mental and physical pain.

Offer staff a place they can go to practise mindfulness in work time when the need arises. Just knowing that there's somewhere quiet that they're allowed to go to centre themselves and regain a more positive frame of mind can make a massive difference. Organisations offering this facility to staff report that the facility is rarely abused and is highly valued. Allowing staff to leave their desk for 10 minutes every now and then can save hours of unproductive time in the office and weeks off sick.

Mindfulness for Service Delivery and Customer Service

Customer service and customer-facing staff are among the most important personnel in organisations nowadays. They're the face of the company, interacting with customers on a day-to-day basis. Top companies appreciate the need for excellence in customer service, and the importance of achieving customer loyalty.

In order to be fully effective in these roles, you need to be fully in the present moment and avoid auto-pilot responses. This can be easier said than done, especially when you're dealing with customers face to face or on the phone all day long, many with similar questions and issues that need addressing. This section provides some mindful strategies for maintaining customer focus, dealing with customer feedback and communicating with clients.

Maintaining customer focus

Maybe you think that you know what your customers want and need, but are you sure? When was the last time you really listened and fully focused your attention on the customer? Many companies focus intensively on customer needs and desires when they're bringing a new product to market, but fail to keep their finger on the customer's pulse as soon as sales targets are being met. Wise companies dig beneath online reviews and recommendations, regularly making opportunities to hear what the customer has to say and act on it to ensure that their products and services continue to meet or exceed customer needs. When interacting with customers (one to one as a customer service representative or when running a focus group), mindfulness can be highly beneficial.

Take a few moments before talking to customers to observe your mental chatter, acknowledging whatever arises, and letting it go kindly without judgement or any further action.

1. **Centre yourself for a few moments by focusing on your breath.**

2. **Focus your attention for the duration of your meeting or phone call entirely on the present-moment experience of assisting, advising or listening to your customer.**

3. **Start with initial questions, but if unexpected things arise, go with them, really listen and reflect on what's said.** This approach is particularly useful if you're running a focus group.

4. **Make sure that the customer feels heard and that their input is valued.** Reflect back and summarise to confirm understanding, especially if the conversation is lengthy or complex.

5. **Check in with yourself regularly to check that you're 100 per cent focused on what's unfolding in the present moment, and that your mind has not wandered to the past or the future.** If your mind has strayed, be kind to yourself — you're only human! Kindly and gently escort your attention back to the present-moment discussion or conversation.

6. **Summarise after the call or meeting what you've gained from your interaction with the customer, and ensure that trends and new ideas are reported back to other areas of the business.** Identify whether you felt any strong emotions during the discussion. Take a moment to explore the impact these had on your thoughts and body.

Dealing with customer feedback mindfully

While most companies have some form of procedure for dealing with complaints, few have a process for dealing with positive feedback.

Dealing with criticism and hostility can be particularly challenging. When people are critical or hostile, feeling threatened is natural, even when you know that it isn't personal, and the customer is far away at the end of the phone line. Most customer service staff have been trained to deal with situations like this in a manner that's professional, polite and that, hopefully, leads to a happy customer. Unfortunately, dealing with difficult customers can take a toll on the staff member, as customer service training rarely shows you how to manage your mind and the importance of self-kindness.

The next time you have to work with a customer who is distressed or angry, try this:

- ✔ **Be as 'fully present' as you can during the conversation.** Remember that, while your product or service may have been the catalyst for their anger or distress, there may be hidden factors driving the intensity of their reaction that may have nothing to do with you, your company or its products.

- ✔ **Be compassionate towards them — think of them as a human in distress.** Adopting this attitude does two things. First, it can help defuse a volatile situation. Second, it reduces your threat response, reducing the pressure you put on yourself. By reducing your threat response, your hormones return to normal and you can think more clearly and act more calmly.

- ✔ **Give yourself a few moments to check in with yourself after the call or meeting to make sure that you're in the right mental and physical shape to deal with the next customer.** Sitting at your desk, starting with your toes and working towards your head, see whether you're holding any tension anywhere. If you find any tension or discomfort, breathe into it on the in-breath, and release it on the out-breath. This small act of self-kindness does two things. First, it allows you to fully release any tension you may still be unconsciously holding (remember that bodily tension can have a major impact on thoughts and mood). Second, it puts you into a more receptive, open, present-moment state for dealing with your next customer interaction, free from the baggage of your last meeting.

If you work in a call centre or in an environment in which you don't have full control of your time, try to use your breaks to recharge your batteries and check in with yourself using the third of the three preceding tips. Taking a few minutes out a few times a day is good for you and good for business. When in a state of (often unconscious) stress, your ability to provide an excellent service to customers is reduced, and you are much more likely to pick up bugs and viruses as your auto-immune system is diminished. Maintain your peak performance with these mini mindfulness exercises.

Communicating mindfully with customers

Mindfulness can be powerful when communicating with others. The same principles apply to your communications with customers, whether face to face or via the phone, email or letter.

When you've just written a letter or email, pause and take a few full breaths before you send it. As you do so, try forgetting the email and everything else and just focus on your breathing. Then read the letter or email from your customer's perspective. (Refer to Chapter 5 for more on mindfulness and communicating with technology.)

Mindfulness for Marketing and PR

In 2013 the job-finding website CareerCast listed 'public relations manager' as the fifth most stressful job in the US. Stress can be helpful, motivating you to strive and achieve more. But it can also cloud your judgement, have a negative impact on your mood, reduce your ability to make good decisions and cause serious illnesses.

In some organisational cultures, stress can be worn as a badge of honour; if you're not seen to be openly stressed, you're judged to be not working hard enough. Similarly, some organisations may encourage a culture of working long hours. Both stress and a poor work-life balance are bad for business. The statistics and research backing this up are hard to ignore.

When you're really busy, stopping and 'doing nothing' — even for five minutes — may seem counter-intuitive. Spending five minutes practising mindfulness can sometimes feel like doing nothing, but in fact you are working hard to develop the neural pathways in your brain associated with directing your attention to where you want it to be, and switching yourself into a more helpful mode of mind. For example, you may want to direct your full attention to communication, consumer trends, culture or your own working methods.

Communicating powerfully

The foundation that underpins powerful communication is a deep understanding of yourself: Your beliefs, perceptions, judgement and intentions.

Humans are strongly motivated by their beliefs. These beliefs are often unconscious, but can override or impede what you consciously intend to do or say. Remaining fully present is impossible unless you understand what's motivating your feelings and behaviour in the moment. Practising mindfulness can help you develop a conscious understanding of your beliefs. This conscious understanding allows you to decide the extent to which your beliefs shape and influence your work.

Although you may think that you see the whole picture, your brain just picks out what it feels is most relevant at any given time and you make up the rest based on past experience and knowledge. If you accept that your perceptions of any given situation are likely to be limited, you can use mindfulness to help train yourself to see more and guess less.

Your judgement also plays a role in how you communicate. Again, this may be unconscious and can be highly damaging, both to yourself and others. When you feel judged harshly by others, your threat system motivates you to take defensive action. Practising mindfulness helps you recognise this response and minimise its harmful impact.

Lastly, but most importantly, you need to ensure that the outcomes you desire from your communication are linked to your intentions. Make sure that you are fully aware of your intentions before you start to communicate, as these intentions gently steer you through your meeting or presentation. Try to remain open to what others are trying to communicate, and what a positive outcome looks like from their perspective.

You need to create a supportive atmosphere where powerful communication can thrive.

Keeping in tune with consumer and cultural trends

However much time you spend reading trade journals and industry reports, try to accept that you'll never be 100 per cent in tune with consumer and cultural trends. A better starting point is accepting a 50–70 per cent level of understanding, and using your eyes and ears to fill in the gaps when working with consumers or conducting market research. Don't forget that, while you only have one mouth, you have two ears and two eyes — use them wisely to see and hear what's unfolding in front of you in the present moment.

When analysing consumer research and sales data, quickly note down your top three observations immediately after reading. Take a mindful minute, or mindful pause (refer to Chapter 3). This mindful pause can take the form of focusing your attention on taking 10 full breaths, or mindfully drinking a hot drink, focusing on nothing but the present-moment sensations, smells and tastes. What you do doesn't matter; the important thing is to quieten your mind, jump fully into the present moment and reduce your state of arousal so that you can view things with a clear, open mind.

Following the mindful pause, revisit the documents and look for any alternative trends or key facts you may have missed. Bear in mind that the researchers or authors of the documents will have interpreted the facts they were presented with according to their own judgement. They may have missed or discarded something that you think is important. Looking at the documents with a beginner's eyes can yield surprising results and aha moments.

Improving responsiveness

When you practise mindfulness, you discover that a distinct difference exists between 'reacting' and 'responding'. *Reacting* is seen as defensive, often based on auto-pilot reactions stored in the fast to react primitive areas of your brain. Reactions are often fuelled by emotions, rather than rational, higher-brain thoughts. *Responding* is altogether more thoughtful. By pausing before acting, you allow yourself time to apply your more powerful higher brain. Responses contain reasoning, and are guided less by emotion and more by logic.

Although responding may seem more passive, a response is more active and can change the direction of an interaction. Practising mindfulness helps you to become more centred and aware of others. By embracing mindful prevention of reacting, you can focus on more beneficial responses that improve your interaction with clients and colleagues alike.

Chapter 7

Integrating Mindfulness with Coaching

· ·

· ·

*M*ost medium- to large-sized organisations now offer coaching for their staff. The reason is simple — coaching is one of the most effective ways of achieving staff development.

Business and executive coaches are increasingly integrating mindfulness into their approach. The early adopters practised mindfulness for many years before the emergence of supporting research gave them the confidence to openly introduce the techniques to their clients. Nowadays, as mindfulness goes mainstream, we find that business coaches are approaching us to help them incorporate the techniques in their own work. Offering ways to help clients fulfil their potential is what coaches are all about, so their own mastery of the techniques creates a win-win situation.

In this chapter we cover the basics of mindfulness coaching. We also talk about overcoming self-doubt and increasing clarity to integrate mindfulness into coaching.

Discovering Mindful Coaching

Mindful coaching is the process of sharing mindfulness-based values and exercises to help individuals or teams to develop both professionally and/or personally. The development occurs as a result of an increased awareness of someone's internal patterns of thoughts and emotions, and their awareness of outer opportunities and challenges.

Traditional coaching was often based on the GROW model developed by Sir John Whitmore:

> **G** — Goals
>
> **R** — Reality
>
> **O** — Options
>
> **W** — What next?

The 'goals' element involves helping the client to discover what he wants to achieve. The client is then asked to reflect on the reality of his current situation. What's actually happening for him right now? Next, he comes up with various options for achieving his goals. In this stage he's asked to let go of self-limiting beliefs by considering questions such as, 'If money was not an issue, what would you do?' Finally, in the 'what next?' stage, the coach asks the client to commit to one or several specific actions that he will take over the next few weeks or months, until the next coaching session.

Several traditional coaching values are shared with mindfulness:

- ✔ Empathy and compassion
- ✔ Curiosity and openness
- ✔ Listening in the present moment
- ✔ Awareness of one's thoughts and emotions
- ✔ Trust and respect
- ✔ Clarity and focus
- ✔ Wisdom and reflection

However, several values are seemingly in conflict with traditional coaching approaches, as shown in Table 7-1.

The traditional coaching model is very much goal-orientated. The basic premise is to find out what you really want to achieve at work, set realistic yet challenging goals and then work at meeting those goals.

Table 7-1	Mindfulness versus Coaching
Mindfulness	*Coaching*
Emphasises acceptance, but gives you the tools to change	Emphasises change
Shift toward being — non-striving	Shift towards doing and action — striving towards goals
The core of your being is whole, complete and well	Emphasis on changing outer circumstances and inner attitudes to reach a sense of wellbeing
Present-moment focus	Future focus
Holistic — sees the big picture; considers the effects of one's actions on others	Self-focused; emphasises personal achievement

Mindfulness goes beyond goals and goal-setting. Rushing too quickly to set goals without reflecting on where you are now, what you notice within and around you and, most importantly, whether such goals are appropriate is a wasteful use of energy. Mindfulness offers the awareness and insight from which goals and their outcomes can emerge. Figure 7-1 shows how mindful coaching combines the best of mindfulness and traditional coaching.

Mindfulness

• Emphasises 'non-doing'

• Present focus

• Values acceptance

Mindful coaching

• Values reflection and action

• Present and future focus

• Values acceptance and change

Traditional coaching

• Action focus

• Future orientation

• No emphasis on acceptance

Figure 7-1: Mindful coaching combines the principles of mindfulness and coaching.

Seeing mindfulness as a coaching toolbox

We hesitate to recommend mindfulness as a 'tool' because present-moment awareness is so fundamental that it underlies all other tools and techniques. For this reason, although you may be considering using mindfulness as a tool with your clients, we suggest that you see mindfulness as a tool box — without mindfulness, you don't have a base from which to use all your other tools.

Mindfulness is useful in coaching because it offers clarity of insight.

The essence of mindfulness is non-judgemental awareness. If you can look at your problems, challenges and difficulties without judgement, you're much better able to see them for what they are. You can then make a decision and take action — which is what coaching is all about.

Figure 7-2 illustrates how mindfulness can underlie the coaching process.

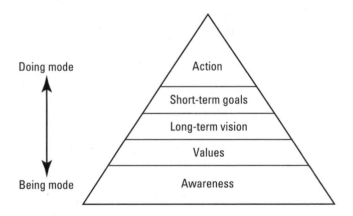

Figure 7-2: Traditional coaching can forget what underlies values and goals — awareness itself.

So, the paradox between mindfulness as associated with non-doing or being, and coaching as to do with doing/action isn't so much a paradox after all. They work together well.

Let's say you're being coached at work. Consider what it would be like to undertake coaching without a deep and full awareness of yourself. You'd set goals that aren't right for you. You'd keep missing opportunities to achieve your goals. And your approach would be mechanical, automatic and unfulfilling as you wouldn't be truly present.

And imagine if, when being coached, you practised mindfulness and non-doing but never set any goals or reflected on your actions. You'd live in the present moment but your achievements in the workplace would be limited. You wouldn't be stretching yourself at all and would probably be bored or unfulfilled — not an ideal state of mind if you're coaching clients.

We think that combining both approaches is best — spending time practising and cultivating mindfulness and time-setting and achieving realistic goals in line with your own values. That's coaching with mindfulness and a great way to work with clients.

Personal practice is crucial if you want to be an effective mindfulness coach. You can't hope to be able to coach others in mindfulness if you're not mindful yourself. When you're mindful yourself, you not only explicitly teach the principles of mindfulness, you also embody mindfulness. And when you embody mindfulness, you send unconscious signals to others about the benefits of mindfulness.

Take a few minutes to listen to a talk by one of the great mindfulness teachers. You can find the following teachers online: Jon Kabat-Zinn, Thich Nhat Hanh, the Dalai Lama, Jack Kornfield or Matthieu Ricard. Tailor your search depending on what you're seeking, such as 'What effect does their tone of voice and ideas have on you?', 'Do they make you feel more calm and present?' or 'Does their talk increase your own level of mindfulness?'

Mindfulness is always much more than a tool, technique or exercise. Mindfulness is a way of living and being.

Applying mindfulness in coaching

You can integrate mindfulness into coaching in lots of different ways. No one way is better than another. You need to identify the needs of your client and use that knowledge to decide how to coach them most effectively with mindfulness.

Different levels of mindfulness can be applied to coaching, as described here:

- ✔ **Level 1: Being mindful as a coach.** This level is the least effective way of offering mindfulness coaching. The coach practises mindfulness exercises regularly in his own life and intends to be fully present with clients when he works with them. He sees the coaching session as an opportunity to be mindful. He doesn't teach any mindfulness in the session as he lacks the training and experience.

- ✔ **Level 2: Bringing in mindful attitudes.** The coach not only practises mindfulness himself but also shares some key attitudes of mindfulness in the coaching session. Mindfulness attitudes include curiosity, self-compassion, compassion for others, acceptance of what can't be changed, recognition of the impermanence of people, events and situations, understanding that people are connected not separate, and valuing your own personal, self-centred goals but also considering their impact on others.

- ✔ **Level 3: Introducing short mindful practices.** The coach actually begins using the word 'mindfulness' and recommends that clients try some mindfulness exercises. He doesn't actually guide mindfulness in the session but does offer a book or guided audio to work through. The coach recommends working through a selection of exercises each week.

- ✔ **Level 4: Guiding mindful exercises in the session.** If the coach is trained in mindfulness, he guides some mindful exercises in the session. Training is particularly important at this stage so that the coach doesn't guide the exercise ineffectively or offer mindfulness to clients when actually they may need some other form of support or guidance.

- ✔ **Level 5: Using most of the session to teach mindfulness.** Most of the session is spent explaining the principles of mindfulness and showing clients ways to implement mindfulness into their work and everyday life. The coach starts and ends the session with guided mindfulness exercises and uses the middle of the session to explore how mindfulness can be applied to the challenges the client is dealing with at work or home.

Shamash trains mindfulness coaches, and ensures they are able to offer up to Level 5 mindful coaching. That way, they have the choice to use approaches that are most relevant for their clients.

If you're looking to train as a mindful coach, ensure you're trained to offer a range of mindfulness exercises to your clients depending on their needs.

No matter what kind of coach or consultant you are, never underestimate the power of simply listening mindfully. Ask open, simple questions such as 'Can you tell me more about that?' or 'Anything else you'd like to say?' and then listen with mindfulness. Leading your clients in this way helps them to be more mindful and can lead to a deep level of transformative insight.

One level is no better than another in this model. If you're a coach, use the right level for you and your client. If you're inexperienced with mindfulness, start with Level 1. If you've been practising mindfulness for years, consider further training in mindful coaching and begin work at levels 4 or 5, if that's what your client needs.

Using Practical Ways to Integrate Mindfulness into Coaching

People seek out coaching to meet a particular need — whether fixing something that's gone wrong or desiring to improve their performance.

Your clients may have a range of problems. They may be overwhelmed with pressure at work. Maybe they're unable to clarify their goals. Perhaps they're lacking in self-confidence and hope that coaching will give them a boost. Or maybe they want to improve their ability to communicate with colleagues at work.

Some clients seek out mindful coaching because they want to improve their performance. Shamash has developed a mind fitness course designed to improve such clients' focus, intelligence and creativity. Mind fitness coaching combines mindfulness with other exercises from positive psychology and guided imagery to help people train their minds just like an athlete trains their body.

This section describes two key benefits of mindful coaching — increased clarity and reduced self-doubt. Obviously many other benefits exist but working on these two introduces you to a few creative ways to use mindful coaching with your clients.

Increasing insight and clarity

Picture a snow globe. You shake it and it fills with imitation snow. When the snowflakes settle, a pretty little village or Christmas scene is revealed.

That snow globe provides a good metaphor for the clarity that can be revealed through mindfulness. Mindfulness gives your clients an opportunity for their frantic thoughts and emotions to settle down. With time, as your clients find out how to step back from their thoughts, they see their own situation with greater clarity and can identify what they need to do to improve it.

Have you had that experience? Have you been so busy with your work and personal life that you couldn't see what you needed to do next? And then, after practising mindfulness exercises or having a nice holiday, free from distractions, have you been better able to see your situation clearly and known how to change things? We think that mindfulness is *the* best approach for increasing a client's clarity and insight.

Mindfulness can lead to clarity and insight in the following ways:

- ✔ Mindfulness exercises give you time to become more aware of your thoughts about various situations at work.

- ✔ Mindfulness makes you become more aware of your feelings about various situations at work.

- ✔ Mindfulness puts you in touch with your bodily sensations, which can lead to 'gut feelings' that are surprisingly accurate.

- ✔ Mindfulness can help your mind calm down. Within that calm, you're better able to see situations for what they are rather than your idea of them.

- ✔ Mindfulness helps you become more accepting and less judgemental, which means that you don't colour work situations and projects with your own issues. Instead, you have the clarity of insight.

Here's another analogy that may work for you. Picture mindfulness as the process of cleaning a window. Mindfulness is the act of cleaning, the dirt on the window represents recurring thoughts about the past and future, and the scene through the window represents the world around you. Each time you work through a mindfulness exercise, the windows of your perception are cleansed and you're better able to see what's in front of you. Without mindful practice and mindful values, the window can easily become a little dirty again and prevent you from seeing what's going on.

Here are a few practical exercises to try with your clients to help them gain greater clarity and insight. You can try these exercises on yourself or your clients:

- ✔ **One minute of silent reflection:** Ask your clients to close their eyes and relax for a few moments. Then tell them to ask themselves, 'How can I best take care of myself?' Tell them to observe any ideas, feelings or emotions that emerge. Then tell them to ask again, 'How can I best take care of myself?' Give your client a minute of silence to reflect on the question.

  You can change the question so that it seems right for your client or yourself.

- ✔ **Mindful movement:** No reason exists why you can't do some mindful movements with your client if you're working one to one. Ask the client's permission and, if willing, guide some short mindful movement exercises. You can use Tai Chi or Qigong, if you're familiar with those disciplines. If not, simply ask clients to stand up and close their eyes. Then, as they feel their breathing, ask them to sweep their arms up and down in front of them for a couple of minutes. Many of our clients enjoy mindful movement more than the sedentary exercises such as mindfulness of breath and mindful pauses (refer to Chapter 3 for more on these).

- ✔ **Switching chairs, switching perspective:** Mindfulness is about stepping back and seeing things from different perspectives. So, if your client is in conflict with a colleague, place an empty chair in the room. Ask the client to imagine a colleague in the chair and to notice his feelings and share his thoughts about the person and situation. Then, ask him to sit in the other chair, imagining that he is his colleague, speaking to himself. Again, ask him to notice his feelings and share his thoughts. This exercise can help clients to step back from their own view of a situation and see things from the other person's perspective.

- ✔ **A touch of frost:** This exercise teaches the power of acceptance versus avoidance. Ask clients to hold a piece of ice in their hands and to try to avoid what they're feeling as much as possible. Suggest that they think about something else other than the discomfort. After a minute, ask your clients to rate how painful they found the experience. Then ask them to practise one minute of mindful breathing and then to hold another piece of ice. This time, they need to accept the sensation. Ask them to feel the sensation together with their breathing. Tell them to allow the sensation to be there, and to almost relax into it. Again, ask them to rate their pain and share their observations and insights. Ask your clients how this experience relates to the challenges they're facing in the workplace. This exercise demonstrates the power of mindful acceptance and often leads to many insights.

Overcoming self-doubt

Self-doubt is a sense of fear or uncertainty about yourself and your ability to achieve something. When Shamash was at university, he was quite shy. He could deal with small groups of people but giving presentations to a roomful of other students made him feel anxious. Around that time, Shamash began to study and practise mindfulness and other ancient Eastern philosophies. As a result, he discovered the danger of believing one's own self-limiting beliefs and discovered how to see them as thoughts rather than facts.

Consider this: If you were absolutely guaranteed to succeed, what would you do with your life? Would you continue to work for the same company or would you apply for a different job? Would you try to get a promotion? Would you quit your job and go travelling around Italy? Asking your clients this question can often lead to interesting answers.

The following exercise helps you to clarify your client's true desires and goals in both their career and personal life, and offers a way to let go of limiting beliefs. Try it yourself first.

1. **Bring yourself into the present moment by focusing your attention on your breath and bodily sensations.**

2. **Ask yourself: 'If I could be successful in anything I chose to do, what would I do?'**

3. **Notice the thoughts, feelings, images and ideas that emerge.** Do you feel excited or nervous? Are you full of ideas or drawing a blank? Whatever emerges is

fine — and interesting! Notice how your mind is reacting to the question.

4. **Refocus your attention on the present moment. Feel a few breaths.**

5. **Ask yourself again: 'If I could be successful in anything I chose to do, what would I do?'**

6. **Notice what happens in your mind. Be fully aware of what emerges in your consciousness.**

7. **Step back from the limiting thoughts and beliefs that make you think you wouldn't succeed; dispense with all the various reasons why your ideal scenario wouldn't work.** Be the observer of those doubts rather than being stuck within them.

8. **Place the thoughts on clouds or into bubbles, or whatever other technique you prefer, to create some distance between you and your thoughts.** Picture doubts as trains that approach a platform and then whizz away.

9. **Refocus your attention each time your mind wanders.** This wandering is fine and perfectly normal. Just kindly bring your attention back when you notice.

10. **Finish the mindfulness reflection with a few mindful breaths.**

Now consider what you discovered. Did you identify your heart's desire? Try to identify the self-doubts or limiting beliefs that are holding you back. Did you enjoy watching them fly away into the distance or did that approach not work for you? Did this exercise make you feel frustrated or curious? If you felt uncomfortable, in what part of your body did such feelings manifest themselves?

Your answers to these questions lead to further insights about yourself and are a step towards experiencing greater self-confidence and less self-doubt.

Hopefully you can see the value of this mindful exercise for your clients. Figure 7-3 shows how such a process can help your clients to step back from their self-limiting beliefs and perhaps achieve goals they previously thought were impossible.

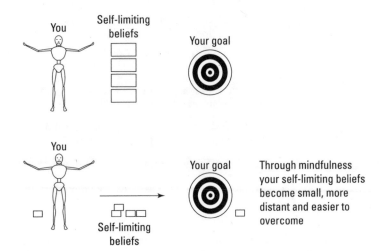

Figure 7-3: The benefits of stepping back from self-limiting beliefs.

There's no right or wrong response to this exercise. Just notice what happens.

For more information on mindful coaching, check out our full-size book, *Mindfulness at Work For Dummies* (Wiley), which has plenty of additional detail about coaching your team and rolling out mindfulness in your organisation, as well as guidance on hiring a mindfulness coach.

Chapter 8

Commissioning Mindfulness Training in the Workplace

*I*ntroducing mindfulness to an organisation can be a daunting experience, but it needn't be. This chapter provides key things to consider when piloting mindfulness within your organisation. If you follow the steps detailed in this chapter you should create a win-win scenario. Your staff benefit, the organisation benefits and you look good for having the idea and following it through. We make a start by looking at the basics.

Bringing Mindfulness Training to Work

There are a number of ways that you could introduce mindfulness to your organisation. This section will help you establish what you hope to achieve, which in turn will help you select the best approach.

Starting with the end in mind

As with all effective personal and professional development initiatives, you should always start with the end in mind. The first question to ask yourself is what outcomes you're hoping to achieve. To put it another way, you need to identify what you hope will be different (in organisational and individual terms) immediately after and in the months following the programme.

Choosing from the menu of possibilities

Mindfulness can help your organisation and your staff in many ways, some of which are easier to evaluate than others. Possible benefits that mindfulness can bring to your organisation include:

- ✔ Improved relationships with colleagues and customers
- ✔ Improved empathy, self-kindness and kindness to others
- ✔ Increased focus and concentration
- ✔ Improved productivity
- ✔ Improved resilience and wellbeing
- ✔ Improved staff engagement
- ✔ Positive changes to brain structure

When you've decided on the most desirable outcomes you're seeking to achieve, you need to state them as learning and development (L&D) outcomes. These desired outcomes can form the basis of discussion with mindfulness trainers, and ensure that those leading the project have a clear idea of what 'success' looks like to you.

Outcomes should always be demonstrable, so they must always be written in behavioural terms. Outcomes are different to aims and objectives. Aims and objectives are usually shared with participants before or at the start of the course. Outcomes are there to help the organisation shape the structure, order and evaluation of the course and aren't normally shared with participants. Think carefully before sharing outcome statements with participants as doing so may positively or negatively impact on the evaluation data. When presented at the outset with the outcomes the organisation wishes to achieve, some participants report overly positive outcomes as they wish to promote mindfulness within the organisation. Others may play down the outcomes for a variety of personal reasons.

Here are a few example outcomes for a taster (introductory) session and full pilot (see the section 'Considering options for introductions and pilots' for more info on these session types), respectively:

Example of outcomes for a mindfulness at work taster session

Your outcome statement may read as follows.

'By the end of the session, participants will:

- ✓ Be able to explain in simple terms what mindfulness is
- ✓ Be able to explain in simple terms how mindfulness works
- ✓ Have experienced some simple mindfulness practices
- ✓ Have developed strategies to transfer what they've learned into the workplace
- ✓ Be keen to find out more about mindfulness, and possibly attend further training'

Example outcomes for a mindfulness at work pilot

Your outcome statement may read as follows:

'By the end of the eight-week course, participants will:

- ✓ Be able to explain what mindfulness is
- ✓ Be able to explain how mindfulness works both from a practical and basic neurological perspective
- ✓ Have practised using a wide range of mindfulness tools and techniques
- ✓ Have applied what they've learned to their work
- ✓ Have improved their productivity (based on self-reporting evaluation measures)
- ✓ Have improved their resilience (based on self-reporting evaluation measures)
- ✓ Demonstrate a more positive outlook (based on staff survey outcomes before and after)'

Building in evaluation

When considering introducing mindfulness (which for some members of staff may be regarded as radical), you need to be able to justify your decision to do so in business terms.

Gathering robust evaluation data relating to measures that matter to your organisation is essential.

Many people make the mistake of trying to bolt on evaluation measures at the end. To really be effective, they should be 'designed in' at the outset. When you've agreed on your outcomes, the mindfulness specialist you're working with should be able to design evaluation measures for your individual mindfulness programme. You can then use these evaluation measures pre- and post-training. You can use an online or corporate survey tool to reduce the work involved. Many free online survey tools do basic analysis of results for you, saving on inputting time and time to complete calculations and statistics. You may find it prudent to make it a condition of attending the course that participants agree to complete both pre- and post-training evaluation questionnaires in a timely manner. Also make sure that participants are happy to have their collective data shared with others in an anonymous format.

Your pre-mindfulness evaluation measures may include:

- A measure of mindfulness, such as the Mindfulness Attention Awareness Scale (MAAS)

- Organisational measures such as 'My organisation is a great place to work' or 'I look forward to coming to work'

- A measure of depression, anxiety and stress using a measure such as the DASS 21 (Depression Anxiety Stress Scales; refer to Chapter 6 for more)

- A measure of self-kindness, such as the one developed by Neff

The post-course evaluation should include the same measures, but you may also wish to include a statement such as:

I feel that mindfulness has helped me ...

1. **Function better when under pressure**

2. **Focus my attention on the task in hand**

3. **Improve the way I manage strong feelings and emotions**

4. **Respond differently to challenges and difficulties at work**

5. **Improve relationships with colleagues**

6. Look after myself better at work

7. Be a more effective employee

(Answer choices = No change; To a small extent; To some extent; To a great extent; Significantly.)

Discuss early on who will be conducting the evaluation. Participants may be more willing to share data with an independent person outside the organisation (such as the mindfulness specialist). This external person can then render the data anonymous before it is presented to the organisation. If the participants know in advance that the answers they provide will be anonymous, they're more likely to be open and honest. Conversely, you, or your learning and development team, may wish to conduct the evaluations yourselves.

One final thing to consider is the most appropriate method for delivering the course. For a taster, or introductory, session a trainer-led approach is generally best. Taster sessions can usually be run by one mindfulness specialist for large numbers of people. However, for mindfulness training purposes, smaller groups are better to allow for discussion and reflection on experiences. Mindfulness can be taught to larger groups with the support of additional trainers.

If your group includes senior managers, they may possibly feel that exploring their reactions and experiences in relation to mindfulness practices is inappropriate in a group setting. In addition, senior managers may not find it easy to attend all sessions and mindfulness training isn't something you can dip in and out of. Senior staff often find one-to-one mindfulness coaching a better learning option.

Considering options for introductions and pilots

You can introduce mindfulness into an organisation in many ways. The correct approach varies from organisation to organisation. Experienced mindfulness specialists should be able to adapt their approach to meet your specific organisational culture and needs, giving your project a greater chance of success. Here are two options to consider.

A packed-lunch session

This kind of session can be a good option for companies where mindfulness training may be met with resistance or where time off for 'personal development' is not a priority. If staff are allowed a 15-minute break in the morning, 30 minutes for lunch and a 15-minute break in the afternoon, these breaks can be combined to create a one-hour slot at lunchtime. Participants can bring their own packed lunch (or you can provide a simple buffet) and eat while listening to an introduction to mindfulness. The introduction may include mindful eating and other quick techniques such as the three-step focus break (refer to Chapter 4) or mindfulness of breath (refer to Chapter 3). At the end of the session, participants should complete a brief paper-based questionnaire, including questions such as:

- I would be interested in attending a mindfulness course. (Strongly disagree; Disagree; Agree; Strongly agree.)

- I think that mindfulness can help me in my work. (Strongly disagree; Disagree; Agree; Strongly agree.)

A half-day session

A half-day session can provide a much more in-depth experience of mindfulness and can form the first part of a longer programme. The half-day session may include:

- Underpinning theory:
  - What mindfulness is
  - The research behind mindfulness
  - Applications of mindfulness
  - The fight-or-flight response
  - Living on auto-pilot
  - The mind–body connection
- Mindfulness practices
  - The raisin exercise
  - Mindfulness of breath
  - Body scan
  - The three-step focus break
- Experiential learning
  - The opportunity to experience mindfulness practices
  - The opportunity to discuss experiences with another participant or the group as a whole, if desired

Administer a short questionnaire at the end of the session to gauge interest and find out whether participants think that mindfulness training is something worth offering more widely or as a full course.

Taking care of the practicalities

A number of practical considerations must be borne in mind when organising a mindfulness taster or full course. First is the *availability of a suitable room*. Ideally, the room should be reasonably private (not one with glass walls that people can stare through, for example). The room should also be reasonably quiet and not too hot or cold. Most mindfulness at work specialists require a fairly standard training room with comfortable chairs, tables and possibly a digital projector, screen and flip chart. Some (but not all) mindfulness trainers require a room with yoga mats, with space for the participants to lie down for some of the mindfulness practices. Some mindful movement exercises use basic yoga techniques. Alternatively, mindful movement can be taught sitting on chairs. Ideally, the mindfulness trainer should have the opportunity to view the training room before they start delivering the course.

For an introductory session for a large number of people, a theatre or cabaret room layout is ideal. When teaching mindfulness to a group of 12–15 people, the room is best set up as a classic 'U', with the trainer at the top. Alternatively, you can use a circle or cabaret-style set-up if space permits. A classroom-style layout, with one small desk per person and everyone sitting apart, is likely to be unsuitable for mindfulness training as it restricts group interaction.

In many organisations members of the learning and development team are responsible for training rooms. Thus a member of this team will probably ensure that the room is set up in advance of the mindfulness trainer arriving. Sometimes the rooms are communal. If so, you need to ensure that the trainer knows how to get the equipment set up, and who to call if they need help.

The next practical consideration is how you *market and publicise the development opportunity to staff*. Is the mindfulness taster or full course 'a personal development opportunity' or 'a professional development opportunity', or both? Is it about staff wellbeing or productivity? Is it about resilience or creativity? You need to be clear about the purpose of the course in the message you send. Also consider the medium of communication: Posters, flyers, emails, messages on the intranet, announcements in staff newsletters and presentations during team briefings are all possibilities. Lastly, consider who's best placed to do what. Mindfulness specialists may be happy to help you develop your promotional materials or even produce a first draft of flyers and intranet content. Don't be afraid to ask for help — being the in-house champion of the project doesn't automatically mean that you're a mindfulness expert!

The final practical consideration is *selection of participants*. If you're running a large-scale mindfulness taster or introduction, selection isn't an issue. However, if you're running a full mindfulness course, you may need to vet participants to ensure that they're suitable. Mindfulness is effective in treating anxiety, depression and stress, but if people are suffering from particularly high levels of any of these problems, they may struggle with the course. One solution is to ask potential participants to complete an assessment tool such as the DASS 21 (refer to Chapter 6). This tool is freely available on the internet. Potential participants whose scores indicate severe or extremely severe depression, anxiety and stress may need to seek a therapeutic version of the course outside of work. When running a full mindfulness course, also consider the mix of people attending to ensure an even balance of job roles and departments. You may also wish to avoid line managers and their direct reports attending the same course.

Give careful consideration to whether *attendance is to be voluntary or compulsory*. Participants will be more engaged in learning if they're doing so voluntarily. Willing participants are more likely to practise the skills at home than those who are coerced into attending. Notable examples exist of mindfulness being taught as part of compulsory programmes, such as for staff with poor attendance records or as part of leadership development. In these cases, many people who would not have attended a course voluntarily have discovered the benefits of mindfulness; indeed, some of them have gone on to become mindfulness champions in their organisations.

Generally, especially if this event is your first attempt at introducing mindfulness into your organisation, starting with volunteers is best.

Working in partnership and managing expectations

Being the mindfulness project leader in your organisation doesn't automatically mean that you have to be an expert on all things mindful. You may need more support from your training provider than you'd normally expect from someone in their position.

Start conversations with potential providers with this fact in mind, and see how much support they're willing to offer and whether they'll partner you in the project. Although mindfulness has come of age, mindfulness in the workplace context is still in its adolescent stage. As pioneers of mindfulness in the workplace, you need to consider whether you can work together to write up and share your data outside the organisation, if all goes well. Your experience adds to the research base and helps other organisations considering mindfulness training. This approach to working should benefit both of you. Make sure that you clearly define who is responsible for what and when, so that you can manage each other's expectations. Remember that you are both in this together and, unlike some box-ticking staff development activities, the outcomes really matter.

Identifying follow-up strategies

Following on from the (hopefully successful) mindfulness introduction, you need to agree what is to happen next. If others need to be involved in making the decision, make a date in their diaries in advance to ensure that you don't lose momentum. Try to get everything in place for the follow-up before you begin the introductory session.

Check out our mindfulness pilot checklist online at www. dummies.com/go/mawessentials for a handy reference to help you plan your pilot session.

Different Approaches to Teaching Workplace Mindfulness

No 'standard' approaches to mindfulness training in the workplace exist, which can make choosing the approach that best suits your organisation's needs rather tricky. The syllabuses of different mindfulness courses can be adapted for use in the workplace. This section provides an outline of four different approaches to teaching mindfulness. The syllabuses for all four are readily available in books or on the internet.

Mindfulness Based Stress Reduction (MBSR)

MBSR was developed in the USA in the 1970s and has been the subject of much research. MBSR and MBCT (Mindfulness Based Cognitive Therapy) are similar and share around 80 per cent of their content. The main difference is that MBSR focuses on treating mental distress (such as stress) in general. MBCT focuses more on *how* a person thinks.

Until fairly recently, MBSR has been mainly used in a clinical setting, helping patients with diverse conditions ranging from stress to chronic pain and tinnitus, to substance abuse. In order to teach MBSR, instructors need to have completed lengthy training. MBSR training is delivered using a well-researched eight-week syllabus developed by Jon Kabat-Zinn.

In order to advertise that they're running an 'MBSR' course, trainers must follow this eight-week syllabus. If training is advertised as 'based on MBSR', it is likely to use key aspects of the established syllabus but may deviate from it or have additions created by the trainer. Adaptations to suit individual client needs will make the latter the case for most workplace courses.

Mindfulness Based Cognitive Therapy (MBCT)

MBCT was developed in the UK in the1990s by Zindal Segal, Mark Williams and John Teasdale. As with MBSR, MBCT was first developed to help people with depression in a clinical setting. The National Institute for Health and Care Excellence (NICE) is an independent organisation, and was set up by the UK government in 1999 to decide which drugs and treatments are available on the National Health Service (NHS) in England and Wales. MBCT is approved in the UK by NICE as a 'treatment of choice' for recurrent depression. MBCT blends mindfulness with aspects of cognitive behavioural therapy and is more focused on helping people find out how to manage their mind than the MBSR approach.

In 2011 Mark Williams (co-creator of MBCT) co-authored with the journalist Danny Penman, *Mindfulness: A Practical Guide to Finding Peace in a Frantic World*. This book contains details of an eight-week MBCT course, adapted for a non-clinical population.

It includes a CD of the mindfulness exercises covered on the course for the readers to practise at home. The exercises each take between eight and 12 minutes, which is less time than traditionally taught on MBCT and MBSR courses. The course also includes practical exercises (such as 'habit releasers'), which aren't part of the core MBCT syllabus. The Williams and Penman course is structured as follows:

- ✔ Week 1: Waking up to the auto-pilot

- ✔ Week 2: Keeping the body in mind

- ✔ Week 3: The mouse in the maze

- ✔ Week 4: Moving beyond the rumour mill

- ✔ Week 5: Turning towards difficulties

- ✔ Week 6: Trapped in the past or living in the present

- ✔ Week 7: When did you stop dancing?

- ✔ Week 8: Your wild and precious life

For further information on this approach, visit the book's website at www.franticworld.com.

'The Mindfulness Exchange' and Juliet's organisation 'A Head for Work', are both major providers of mindfulness in the workplace training, and are leading the way in developing William and Penman's approach. Both base their workplace mindfulness training on the eight-week course described in the book. For information on these two providers, visit www.mindfulness-exchange.com or www.aheadforwork.co.uk.

If you're looking for an online eight-week mindfulness course try www.livemindfulonline.com, recently developed by Shamash. It includes lots of videos, downloadable audios, mindful exercises, weekly emails and an online community, combining both MBSR and MBCT.

Mindfulness At Work Training (MAWT)

MAWT is a five-week mindfulness course developed by the authors of this book based on MBCT, with the addition of specific applications of mindfulness in the workplace.

Weeks 1–2 cover the key aspects of mindfulness usually taught on weeks 1–4 of an MBCT course. Weeks 3–5 apply mindfulness to key work challenges, and include some aspects taught on weeks 5–8 of an MBCT course. As with MBCT and MBSR, home practice is an essential component, with short exercises (around 10 minutes each) included. A MAWT course is structured as follows:

- ✔ Week 1: Understanding mindfulness at work
- ✔ Week 2: Working with the body in mind
- ✔ Week 3: Mindful communication at work
- ✔ Week 4: Mindfully working with difficult people and strong emotions
- ✔ Week 5: Mindful working in times of change

Visit www.mawt.co.uk for more information.

Search Inside Yourself (SIY)

SIY was developed by Chade-Meng Tan (known as Meng), one of the first engineers to be hired at Google. When Google allowed engineers to spend 20 per cent of their time pursuing their own passions, Meng decided that he wanted to help his workmates nurture emotional intelligence through the practice of mindfulness. Meng worked with a range of people including emotional intelligence expert Dan Goleman, mindfulness trainers, psychologists and a CEO. He ultimately created a seven-week personal growth programme. SIY was launched in 2007, and since then more than 1,000 employees have participated in SIY courses with excellent results.

In 2012 Meng decided to make the principles and components of SIY available to companies everywhere and published them in his book, *Search Inside Yourself: The Unexpected Path to Achieving Success, Happiness (and World Peace)*. His programme focuses on the five key domains of emotional intelligence — self-awareness, self-regulation, motivation, empathy and social skills — and integrates mindfulness practice, science and leadership applications at all levels. In the example below, SIY is taught via three modules:

✔ SIY 101: Introduction to emotional intelligence (2 hours)

✔ SIY 102: Day of mindfulness (7 hours, prerequisite: SIY 101)

✔ SIY 103: Developing the five domains of emotional intelligence (10 hours, prerequisite: SIY 101)

To find out more about this approach to teaching mindfulness coupled with emotional intelligence, invest in a copy of Meng's book or visit www.siyli.org.

Hiring an Experienced Mindfulness Practitioner

Unlike many development courses routinely offered to staff by organisations, mindfulness isn't an abstract concept that can be quickly learned from a book and translated into a course delivered by a member of the learning and development team. Even attending an eight-week course does not equip you to teach mindfulness to others.

A large amount of what is taught by mindfulness trainers is directly in response to individual participant needs. This aspect of teaching mindfulness can't be covered by any book or by attending one course. It relies on a deep understanding of mindfulness gained over years of practising it, not to mention regular supervision from an even more experienced trainer. This section gives you the information you need to choose the mindfulness trainer best suited to your organisation.

Checking out credentials

No specific standards currently exist for trainers who teach mindfulness in the workplace. Good practice suggests that, as a minimum, trainers teaching mindfulness in the workplace should:

✔ Have good knowledge of the type of organisation that the training will be delivered in or, better still, work experience in the sector

✔ Have good knowledge of and skills in teaching adults in the workplace

✔ Have in-depth knowledge of the mindfulness content and underpinning theory gained through attending courses, self-directed learning and attending seminars in related subject areas

✔ Have followed well-established, regular mindfulness practice for at least 12 months prior to attending teacher training

✔ Have attended a recognised teacher training course (based on MBSR, MBCT or similar), with a minimum duration of 12 months; this course can include both face-to-face teaching and web-based learning or tuition

✔ Be engaged in regular supervision sessions with suitably experienced mindfulness trainers to encourage personal reflection and further development

When we were at school, some of our teachers were excellent at their job and others were terrible! They were all qualified and had done the necessary training. You may find the same with mindfulness teachers. Read their CVs and other credentials with a pinch of salt rather than as an ultimate guide to their competency. We have both met many mindfulness teachers that wouldn't meet the preceding credentials but are excellent teachers, seem to have a natural ability to be mindful, and have years of experience. We have also met highly trained mindfulness teachers who need more training and experience, and quite a number who can't translate mindfulness for a corporate audience. Take time to meet the teacher, get to know them, and discuss your needs at length before hiring them.

Clarifying organisational experience

At present, mindfulness teacher training is generic and not tailored to workplace delivery. Many fine mindfulness trainers with years of experience may struggle to adapt their mindfulness training to the needs and constraints of individual organisations. Some of the methods currently taught routinely in mindfulness teacher training may not sit well in an organisational setting. For this reason, checking out potential trainers' understanding of the business sector that you operate in is important. Make sure that your chosen mindfulness trainer uses language, analogies and methods that sit well with your audience.

Judging compatibility

When selecting a mindfulness trainer for your organisation, try to select one who is happy to adopt a partnership-working approach. Being open and honest is important so that you can establish a collaborative means of working built on trust.

Your chosen trainer should feel comfortable wearing several hats. She may need to help you write flyers and publicity material. Maybe she can assist you in designing, administering or even managing the evaluation process. If she'll be required to send emails directly to participants (for example, welcoming them to the course, confirming home practice or chasing evaluation completion), you need to be sure that she uses appropriate corporate language. Think carefully about what you require from your mindfulness trainer at the outset to manage expectations.

Agreeing on what's possible

When you enter into discussion with a mindfulness trainer for the first time, do so with an open mind. Let the trainer discuss what mindfulness can do for you and your organisation — possibilities may exist that you haven't yet considered. Make sure that the trainer is fully aware of what's important for you. Doing so early on in the process helps you both identify whether any of the outcomes you desire are unachievable. Discovering this at the outset is much better than later in the process. Also agree early on how success will be measured, both in training terms and in relation to organisational outcomes.

When selecting a mindfulness trainer, look for one who ideally has sector experience and thus understands how your staff work and the pressures they may be under. Make sure that the trainer has attended recognised mindfulness teacher training, and by the time she reaches you has had a minimum of two years' personal experience of practising mindfulness. Make sure that she's flexible in her approach, and willing and able to wear several hats to help you during the critical phase of piloting mindfulness within your organisation.

Chapter 9

Thriving on the Challenges of Leadership

- -

In This Chapter

▶ Flourishing in your leadership role

▶ Boosting your resilience using mindfulness

▶ Discovering how you can become a more mindful leader

▶ Leading your organisation mindfully

- -

*M*ost people spend a huge amount of their time at work. It stands to reason, therefore, that work should make you feel good about yourself, give you a sense of personal mastery and be fun. Unfortunately, many people find work to be stressful, demotivating and frustrating. Great leaders identify what motivates people and match their skills to those needed by the organisation, thus creating a win-win situation. In order to create this situation, leaders need to be in a fit state to lead others.

In this chapter we take a look at leadership roles and how to use mindfulness if you're in one!

Understanding Different Leadership Theories

Ideas about what makes a good leader have changed dramatically over time. Most recently, *contingency theories* (such as situational leadership) argue that no one leadership style is correct and that as a leader you need to adopt the correct leadership style for the situation. *Transformational theories* view leaders as agents of change. As a transformational leader you can 'transform' the workplace via teamwork or team development, or by acting as an agent of change or a strategic visionary.

Human potential theories are the latest development and are concerned with the performance of the leader from a human perspective. These theories incorporate authentic leadership, resonant leadership, mindful leadership and neuro-leadership. Human potential theories are concerned with maximising your potential as a leader by being true to your values, and finding out how to work in harmony with yourself rather than trying to be something you're not. Mindfulness is a core element of human potential theories of leadership.

We live in a VUCA world — **v**olatile, **u**ncertain, **c**omplex and **a**mbiguous. This new world may go part of the way to explaining why some leadership theories are no longer effective. Yet many leaders, and you may be one of them, continue to base their leadership behaviours on outdated models. Why? Because like everyone else you probably do a fair amount of your work on auto-pilot.

Adopting new, human potential theories of leadership can be scary, as you discard the security blanket of your old methods of leadership and take a leap into the unknown of being yourself, and maximising your potential as a leader. In this brave new world, you need self-knowledge and the courage to be true to yourself. In return, you can shed the heavy burden of trying to be someone who you are not in favour of being the best you can be.

Thriving Rather Than Surviving

Being a leader is a challenging role, especially in times of recession and economic crisis. Being a senior leader can also be a lonely and isolating experience. At times when you feel under pressure and uncertain about the future, you'll find keeping your team motivated and engaged tough. As a leader, you may also feel less inclined to seek support and guidance from your peers. Catastrophising as thoughts spiral round and round in your head is all too easy.

Imagine missing a report deadline at work. In reality this situation is hardly life or death, is it? But your mind is likely to make up its own story about what's going on, blowing the matter out of all proportion. As you discovered in Chapter 4, your caveman threat response can have a serious impact on your performance, health and happiness. By practising mindfulness and learning to observe thoughts as mental processes, you can change things.

Take the example of Dave and Ken, two middle managers from the same organisation. Both applied for the same senior leadership role. An external candidate was appointed, so neither got the job. How they dealt with the situation was very different.

Dave's thoughts started to spiral down as he catastrophised about the situation. He tried to get on with work, but his mind kept on wandering to what went wrong at the interview, and how this might threaten his career.

Ken, however, applied mindfulness to his feelings of failure and rejection. He noticed himself starting to spiral down and his body becoming tense. He practised mindfulness for a short while, calmly observing his thoughts without reacting or thinking about them further, recognising the impact of his thoughts on his emotions, and then noticing how his body felt. He released the tension he felt and then focused his attention on the present-moment sensation of breathing. Ken returned to his work. He acknowledged feeling sad and a little angry about missing the promotion, but did not let these thoughts and emotions have a negative impact on his work and wellbeing.

This example graphically illustrates how mindfulness can help you, as a leader, pick yourself up after a disappointment and avoid falling into a downward spiral of despair. Mindfulness also teaches you that the problem is never the real problem. Your perception and response to life's challenges is what can throw you out of the frying pan and into the fire!

While many things are beyond your control at work, you always have a choice about how you respond. Choosing how you respond is empowering — it hands control back to you.

Leadership can be challenging, and it's easy to forget to look after yourself. Here are three simple exercises that can help you balance work demands with the need to care for your wellbeing.

Soaking in the good

Think about the little things that make you feel good in life. Examples may include holding a pet, hugging a loved one, someone appreciating something you've done, or seeing the first flowers of spring.

Ask yourself if you can give these small pleasures a little extra attention. As you experience them, try pausing for a moment to really soak in the good they provide. Allow your body time to release feel-good hormones so that you can derive maximum benefit from these pleasurable experiences.

Smiling

When you smile, you're telling your body that everything is fine. This simple action turns off your threat system. Your body immediately stops pumping adrenaline around itself, your blood pressure drops and feel-good hormones such as serotonin are released.

Being kind to yourself

Do you find it easier to demonstrate empathy and kindness to others rather than yourself? Maybe you dismiss the idea of self-kindness as selfishness?

Sometimes you need to be selfish for your own preservation. Try to avoid beating yourself up for mistakes you make, things you get wrong or things you should have done. Being kind to yourself can help reduce or eliminate the detrimental effects of fear, guilt and shame.

Taking a time-out to consciously accept yourself and make friends with the person you really are helps you increase your happiness and creativity. This time-out is especially important if you're a leader. Self-acceptance also helps to train your brain to work in approach mode rather than avoidance mode. A befriending exercise such as 'Cultivating kindness' in Chapter 4 helps you to deactivate your threat system, making it easier to concentrate and gain a fresh perspective. Befriending yourself can be really hard when you first practise it, but it does get easier over time and is definitely worth working on.

For leaders, the ability to identify and overcome outdated mental programming without triggering the threat system is vital. If you're really serious about being a better leader, and thriving rather than surviving, you need to prioritise time to learn mindfulness and embed practice into every day you spend at work.

Being a More Mindful Leader

Human potential models of leadership all centre around the concept of being the best you can be, maximising your innate leadership qualities while being true to yourself and your values. All human potential theories incorporate mindfulness in some shape or form.

This section briefly explores models and ideas around becoming a more mindful leader.

Authentic leadership

Authentic leaders are leaders who demonstrate the genuine desire to understand their own leadership behaviour in order to serve the needs of the organisation and its staff most effectively. Their behaviour and decisions are based on strongly held values and beliefs. By upholding these values and beliefs, they increase their personal credibility and win the respect and trust of their team, colleagues and peers.

Authentic leaders actively encourage collaboration and the sharing of diverse viewpoints, leading in a way that others perceive and describe as 'authentic'. Authentic leadership is all about leaders as individual people. It can be likened to a self-awareness approach to leadership and leadership development.

According to Bill George, former CEO of Medtronic and author of *Authentic Leadership* (Jossey-Bass, 2004), authentic leaders are motivated by their mission, not your money. They tap into your values, not your ego. They connect with others through their heart, not their (sometimes artificial) persona. Authentic leaders should live their lives in such a way that they would be proud to read about their behaviour on the front page of their local newspaper.

George defines authentic leadership as having five dimensions. Authentic leaders:

- ✔ Understand their purpose
- ✔ Practise solid values
- ✔ Lead with the heart
- ✔ Establish connected relationships
- ✔ Demonstrate self-discipline

He believes that acquiring these five dimensions isn't a sequential process, but happens throughout a leader's life, often over a long time.

Mindfulness is a key element of authentic leadership. It underpins all five dimensions described in the preceding bullet list. It helps leaders increase their self-awareness and self-regulation. It helps them to be kinder to themselves and to protect their values.

This activity will give you an indication of how 'authentic' your leadership style is.

Score the following questions as follows: 0 = not at all like me; 1 = a little like me; 2 = mostly like me; 3 = an accurate description of me.

1. **I actively seek feedback to improve the way I communicate and work with others.**

2. **I always say exactly what I mean.**

3. **My actions are always fully consistent with my beliefs.**

4. **I always listen very carefully to others' views and opinions before reaching a conclusion.**

5. **If asked to do so, I can quickly and easily give a true description of how others view my strengths and weaknesses as a leader.**

6. **I never play games — what you see is what you get.**

7. **As a leader, I feel that I need to model behaviours that are consistent with my beliefs.**

8. **I recognise that others may not share my views on life and leadership, and I'm open to others' ideas.**

9. I understand what motivates me, and the values that underpin my work as a leader and my life in general.

10. If I make a mistake I always admit to it and am ready to take full responsibility.

11. My values and beliefs have a huge impact on the decisions I make.

12. I actively seek out others' views to challenge the way I think about things.

Enter your scores in the following table:

Authentic leadership traits							*Score for trait*
Self-awareness	1		2		3		
Transparency and openness	4		5		6		
Embodiment of values	7		8		9		
Seeking a balanced perspective	10		11		12		
Total overall score							

Interpret your trait score as follows:

0 = A trait you do not display or do not value

1–3 = A trait you can work to improve

4–6 = A trait you display

7+ = A trait you truly embody

To work out your overall score, add up the figures in the right-hand column. The authenticity of your leadership style is as follows:

0–13 = A low level of authentic leadership behaviours displayed

14–26 = A moderate level of authentic leadership behaviours displayed

27–36 = Someone who leads with authenticity

If possible, repeat the exercise with one or more colleagues, peers or members of your team. Don't forget to emphasise the need to be honest! Do your team members see you in the same way that you see yourself?

Resonant leadership

Resonant leaders are individuals who manage their own and others' emotions in ways that drive success.

The idea behind resonant leadership is that, rather than constantly sacrificing themselves to workplace demands, leaders should find out how to manage these challenges using specific techniques to combat stress, avoid burnout and renew themselves physically, mentally and emotionally. Many of these techniques are derived from mindfulness practices.

Resonant leaders:

- ✔ Are highly self-aware
- ✔ Demonstrate a high level of self-management
- ✔ Are highly socially aware
- ✔ Are emotionally intelligent
- ✔ Actively work to manage their relationships

Mindful leadership

The latest thinking on effective leadership suggests that leaders need self-awareness (a clear idea of what makes you tick, your strengths, weaknesses, beliefs and motivations) and must be well-grounded and centred.

In addition, leaders need to be able to manage how their mind deals with multiple demands and constant connectivity so that they can maintain peak performance and wellbeing.

Mindfulness helps you to manage your mind by regulating and focusing your attention, making you more aware of your thoughts and emotions. Dan Siegel, clinical professor of psychiatry at UCLA School of Medicine and co-director of the Mindful Awareness Research Center, refers to mindfulness practice as 'good brain hygiene', which is as important to your health as brushing your teeth.

Practising Mindful Leadership

As you process the continuous stream of information coming in from the world around you, your brain selects the things it deems most relevant and often dismisses the remainder. Academics and researchers argue that business performance is strongly influenced by this continuous stream of individual and organisational 'meaning-making'.

Mindfulness encourages a state of active awareness, openness to new information and willingness to view situations from multiple perspectives. Adopting a mindful attitude allows you to suspend judgement until you have all the facts. Doing so refines your 'meaning-making processes', giving you a more balanced view of the world around you.

This state of active awareness can't be achieved by simply grasping the idea of mindfulness as an intellectual concept. To fully benefit from mindfulness, you need to regularly apply it to your workday practices. When you gain sufficient knowledge and confidence, you can help others around you by introducing a few simple mindfulness practices into their working lives. Here are some practical ways to incorporate mindfulness into your work as a leader.

Making mindful decisions

If you've been in a leadership or management role for any period of time, you're probably well versed in various models of decision-making. What you may not be familiar with is looking at your mindset and unconscious mental programming when making decisions. Your thoughts have a huge impact on how your body feels (for example, tension) and your emotions (for example, happiness and fear). Similarly, holding tension or anger in your body has an impact on your thoughts. This impact is often unconscious, but it can have a profound effect on the decisions you make.

A number of researchers have concluded that, when making decisions, emotions and negative information have a huge influence. Surprisingly, numeric information, analytics and logical arguments often have less impact. Refer to Chapter 2 for more on the benefits of mindful decision-making.

By practising mindfulness you become more aware of the different factors at play when making a decision, including the impact of your own meaning-making process, which leads to less subjectivity in decision-making.

Try this activity to improve your approach to making decisions. Follow these steps:

1. **Spend a few moments centring yourself in the present moment.** Focus on the sensation of breathing to make you relax and exist in the present moment.

2. **Clearly define the decision that you need to make.** Close your eyes, or hold them in soft focus (eyes looking down and three-quarters closed). Just sit with the question, using it as an anchor for your attention. Avoid the temptation to start making the decision or to think about it in any way; just keep on repeating the question in your mind.

3. **Imagine the question to be answered placed on a workbench in front of you for closer examination and study.** Spend a few moments exploring it, with kindness and curiosity. Consider:

   • Any negative information you may have associated with the decision — observing how this negative information impacts on your thoughts or emotions

   • Your emotional state in the present moment

   • Any key numerical or statistical information that you may have

4. **Open your eyes, evaluate all the information you have to hand and make your decision.** You can now make a decision taking into account all the factors involved and being fully aware of any bias you may have initially felt.

Communicating ideas and expectations

This book contains lots of information about mindful communication. The key thing to remember is that you're likely to spend a great deal of time on auto-pilot. You may be physically in the same room as the person you're communicating with, but at some point your mind is likely to wander elsewhere. As a leader, you need to make a real effort to be 100 per cent present when communicating. You need to train your brain to notice when your mind wanders to the past or future or to matters unrelated, and gently bring it back to the present moment. In this state of present-moment awareness, you're better able to pick up verbal and non-verbal cues from your audience. You're better able to identify emerging areas of support and build on them. Similarly, you can pick up on areas of dissent and take time to explore or address them. Most importantly, people feel that you're really listening to them and that you value their time and input.

Mindfully encouraging others to speak up and contribute

A key part of being a leader is encouraging people to voice their thoughts and contribute to discussions and meetings. When you're in a mindful, present state of mind, you're better able to encourage people to share their ideas and support them in working collaboratively.

To improve the quality of your meetings, follow these steps:

1. **Remove anything that causes a distraction.** At the start of a meeting or collaborative working session, ask people to switch off their phones and so on.

2. **Set the tone for the meeting or working session.** You need to set the scene:

   • State clearly and concisely what you're trying to achieve.

   • Gain consensus from everyone present.

   • Reassure people that you're open to hearing their opinions and ideas (there's no such thing as a stupid question or suggestion). Back up this statement by making sure that you acknowledge and capture in writing every idea put forward.

   • Do not openly criticise someone's input (whatever you secretly think of it). Value that person by acknowledging their contribution.

3. **Create opportunities for everyone to share ideas and thoughts.** Don't expose people or put them on the spot. If they're initially too shy to contribute, be gentle and supportive.

4. **Recap what has been discussed and decided on so far to maintain direction and momentum.** At regular intervals, pause and give a brief overview.

5. **Make the final decision.** Remember that you're the leader and that the final decision rests with you. If this decision is different to group consensus, always ensure that you thank everyone for their contribution, and let them know that you've really heard and considered their input.

Solving problems mindfully

Defaulting to old ways of thinking and behaving is all too easy when you're trying to solve problems — after all, they've served you well in the past.

Mindful problem-solving takes a more holistic approach.

1. **Take steps to ensure that you're fully in the present moment.** Spend a few minutes doing a short mindfulness exercise of your choice, with your eyes closed or in soft focus.

2. **Place the problem you wish to solve on your 'workbench' of the mind.** Try to picture the scene if you can. Observe how it makes your body feel and any emotions it invokes. Try your best not to judge these feelings and emotions as good or bad — just sit with them.

3. **Ask yourself questions.** After asking each of the following questions, observe the challenge sitting on your workbench and wait for an answer. Acknowledge each answer as it arrives.

   • How/why has the challenge arisen?

   • What factors are involved?

   • What are the possible solutions?

4. **Observe your answers with kindness and curiosity.** Avoid the temptation to drift away from the present moment by focusing on your answers. Observe any strong reactions that are elicited by any part of your exploration. Are you experiencing an emotion? For example, excitement or fear. Is your body responding with a clenched jaw or fluttering in your stomach?

5. **Open your eyes and make a decision on the best way to solve the problem.** You can now make an informed and dispassionate decision, having considered all the facts.

6. See the problem as a challenge. Research suggests that by reframing problems as positive challenges to learn and overcome, you're more likely to take a proactive approach and find effective solutions.

After practising mindfulness regularly for eight weeks or longer you should be able to use techniques like this one much more rapidly, as you develop the ability to quickly tune into the present moment and observe things more objectively.

Creating a Positive and Inspiring Workplace Culture

As a leader, you're the one who sets the tone in the workplace. Being true to yourself and your values is important; that is, you need to be authentic.

If you truly value people's creativity and innovation, make sure that working practices reflect and celebrate these aptitudes. For example, your company could set up a system that identifies and rewards staff who are innovative. Google staff are allocated time each week to work on their pet projects or ideas that interest them.

If you value mindfulness and want to cultivate a more mindful workplace, consider:

- Offering staff mindfulness training in work time.

- Setting aside space for people to get away from their desks or work areas to clear their minds and grab a few moments of mindfulness. Leading organisations are creating these spaces, and this privilege is highly valued and rarely abused.

- Cultivating a culture in which staff feel comfortable leaving their work area for a short time to practise mindfulness somewhere quiet.

- Offering mindfulness drop-in sessions, possibly at lunchtime, which people can join as and when they want to.

As Mahatma Gandhi famously said, 'Be the change you want to see.' If you want to encourage openness and honesty, be open and honest yourself. Many leaders paint a vivid vision of what an organisation is like to work for, but fail to follow this vision through by making sure that the fundamentals are in place to make the vision a reality.

Mindfully take a long hard look at your organisation, and what it looks like from an employee's perspective. Does it really match up to the vision painted of it? Ask yourself what you can do to change things for the better, embodying your beliefs and values.

Chapter 10

Leading People, Change and Strategy

- - - - - - - - - - - - - - - - - - - -

In This Chapter

▶ Leading in the midst of constant change

▶ Helping your organisation flourish

▶ Developing a mindful organisation

- - - - - - - - - - - - - - - - - - - -

*L*eading people and change are arguably the two most demanding aspects of a leader's work. This chapter explores how mindfulness can transform the leadership of people and change, and how the organisation can become more mindful while still keeping a keen eye on the bottom line.

Leading Mindfully when Change is the Norm

In the recent past, change projects at work were managed on the assumption that they had a distinct beginning, middle and end. Arguably the most widely known model says that after the initial shock and denial stage comes a feeling of loss, and in the final stage people start to experiment with the idea of doing something in a new way, eventually embrace it, and the new way of working becomes 'business as usual'. This model is great to bear in mind when major change happens occasionally, and there's time to embed changes and return to a state of business as usual.

Another commonly used model proposes that in the initial stages of change an organisation prepares for change by breaking down old structures and ways of working, which causes uncertainty. In the middle stage, employees work to resolve the uncertainty and look for new ways to do things, and start to support and embrace the desired change. In the final stage (when people have embraced the change) comes further work to embed the new way of doing things into everyday business.

The problem with both models is that the pace of change for many organisations is now so rapid that there's rarely time to complete stage three (embedding and business as usual) before the next change is necessary. So just as the sense of loss and uncertainty starts to recede and people start to explore new ways of doing things, they're plunged straight back into shock, denial and breaking down what they've only just built up.

With little time for 'business as usual', one change follows another and another, so little if any time exists to consolidate and embed each change. Constant, 'bumpy change' requires a new approach to leading change initiatives, centred on human processes of habit formation.

While many change management projects focus on the steps necessary for organisational change, the Prosci ADKAR model focuses on five actions and outcomes necessary for successful individual change, and therefore successful organisational change. In order for change to be effective, individuals need:

- ✔ Awareness of the need for change
- ✔ Desire to participate and support the change
- ✔ Knowledge on how to change
- ✔ Ability to implement required skills and behaviours
- ✔ Reinforcement to sustain the change

Knowledge and practice of mindfulness, together with some basic knowledge of how the brain works, on the part of both the leader and employees makes this model even more effective. In the words of Jon Kabat-Zinn, father of Mindfulness Based Stress Reduction (MBSR), 'You can't stop the waves, but you can learn to surf.'

Try these tips to make dealing with change less challenging:

- ✔ Use mindfulness to help you to identify your unconscious habits and thinking patterns. Decide whether they're serving you well and, if not, consciously work to find new ways of acting and thinking. Repeat these over a two- to three-month period to form new dominant ways of thinking and acting that are more productive.

✔ Use the ADKAR model next time you start to plan for an organisational change. Visit www.change-management.com for more information.

✔ Habits take time to form, so organisational changes may be slow to be adopted. Help employees form new habits by providing opportunities to discuss, experiment with and practise new ways of thinking, behaving and working over a 8–12 week period. The more new habits are practised, the stronger the neural pathways in people's brains become and the easier repeating the 'habit' is.

✔ Staff facing redundancy need just as much support as staff making the transition to the new way of working. Mindfulness training can help those being made redundant deal with the challenges that they're facing, giving them back a sense of control.

Creating Strategies that Allow the Organisation to Flourish

In order to keep pace with change, you need to adapt your strategies. If you want to get ahead of change, a more strategic approach is needed. You have to anticipate trends and proactively define new and innovative ways to move forward. In order to do so, you must be agile and authentic.

Agility is now an essential leadership skill. The increasing speed of change demands that organisations need to become more nimble and flexible. Your ability to spot change on the horizon, anticipate what may happen next and develop strategies in advance is vital.

Authenticity is another essential skill in times of volatile, unpredictable change. Your ability to create clarity by describing your vision and painting a picture of the future is more important than ever. You need to be able to lead with confidence and have the courage to take a stand. You need to build trust and confidence within your teams and be genuine in your communications. Change tends to cause anxiety and confusion. Your role as a leader is to bring a level of certainty about the new direction and evoke a sense of purpose for your staff.

Identifying organisational culture

If you really want to make radical changes to the way your organisation operates, you need to gain a good understanding of its culture.

What's your culture?

There are many tools and models available to help you identify the characteristics of your organisation's culture.

You might wish to use 'cultural dimensions', a framework for cross-cultural communication pioneered by Geert Hofstede and discussed practically in 'Riding the Waves of Culture' by Fons Trompenaars and Charles Hampden-Turner. Alternatively, you might wish to consider the 'Cultural Web', a tool to help align your organisation's culture with strategy, developed by Gerry Johnson and Kevan Scholes in 1992.

An alternative way to work on cultural change is to identify sub-cultures that may exist within an organisation and investigate why they may find it difficult to inter-relate. Rapid and constant change has a huge impact on organisational culture and can result in a *non-culture*, which is a kind of vacuum left where a cohesive culture used to exist. This vacuum needs to be filled with a new collective coherence.

Mindfulness, as you know, helps you to step into the present moment and see what's really going on. This ability is useful when seeking to identify sub-cultures. You need to map the sub-cultures that exist and how these relate to each other. For example, manufacturing may have a completely different sub-culture to finance. Once identified, take time to celebrate the sub-cultures and encourage them to flourish. The idea behind this move is that you bring them out into the open and thus have a better chance of understanding what you're dealing with. Trying to make a sub-culture comply with a corporate ideal often pushes it further underground, which makes it impossible to change. Giving people a unique sub-culture that they can be proud of often encourages that sub-culture to move closer to corporate intent.

Where a weak and dysfunctional sub-culture exists, try to give it a helping hand. Weak sub-cultures can seriously undermine organisational cohesion. Identify why confidence has been lost and help the business area add value to the organisation again.

The final stage of the process involves weaving together the diverse sub-cultures. By getting members of staff from different cultures working together on areas of common purpose, more areas of shared beliefs emerge. The shared cultural beliefs encourage sub-cultures to bond and form a web of shared beliefs. These webs can become strong, and equally as effective as the tightly woven, singular company culture of the past.

Remember that cultural change initiatives take time to embed — no quick fixes exist. As a leader, getting to grips with organisational culture can be the deciding factor between a strategy's or change initiative's success and failure. Ignore organisational culture at your peril! Be mindful that not all organisational cultures may be to your liking. Unless they're seriously detrimental to the organisation, you need to let go of your personal feelings on the matter and spend your energy on getting the different sub-cultures to work together and establish more areas of common ground.

Mindfully discovering common ground

Most researchers believe human beings are more hardwired to cooperate than to compete. Gather together workers from different sub-cultures to work together on areas of common ground. Start the meeting with a three-step focus break (refer to Chapter 4), explaining that participants will be working together for the next few hours, you want them to gain the most from this time and that this technique helps them clear their minds and enables them to do so. Get each participant to write down five things they feel need work — each written on a different piece of paper. Gather the pieces of paper and group them into themes and areas of commonality. These areas of common ground are the things to work on first.

Creating a collective vision for the future

Large organisations generally spend a considerable amount of time and effort on developing organisational visions. Branding and communication experts are drafted in to help the top team define their vision for the future in a manner that will motivate staff and inspire belief, confidence and desire in customers. Smaller organisations sometimes suffer from having no vision, or a vision that is too wordy, difficult to remember and feels unachievable. Visions are intended to paint a vivid picture of the organisation and where it's heading. Less is often more! You need to make your organisational visions memorable and inspiring, but also achievable.

Try using the following steps to help you develop a vision for the future.

Step 1: Centring and visioning.

1. **Settle yourself in a room where you won't be disturbed.** Switch off your mobile phone, your laptop (or at least the volume) and silence any device that may take your attention away from the task at hand.

2. **Sit in a comfortable, upright position.** Close your eyes or hold them in soft focus.

3. **Spend three minutes or so focusing your attention on the sensation of breathing.** Really feel the present-moment sensations of the breath entering your body and the breath leaving your body.

4. **Spend a further three minutes reconnecting with your body in this moment in time.** Check how your feet are feeling at this moment, followed by your legs, bottom, shoulders and head.

5. **Open your eyes and capture on a piece of paper or your laptop the five key characteristics representing how you'd like your organisation to be in three to five years' time.** You can express these characteristics as words, pictures or paragraphs of descriptive text.

Step 2: Identifying things you need to start, stop and continue doing.

1. **Refocus your attention on the present-moment experience.** Try to let go of the thoughts that are probably rattling round in your head. Remember, you've jotted them down, so nothing important will be forgotten.

2. **Spend two minutes focusing your attention on the thoughts in your mind**. Observe them as mental processes and then let them go.

3. **Spend a further two minutes focusing your attention on your breathing, as described in Step 1.**

4. **Open your eyes.** Read the 'five characteristics' you jotted down in Step 1 and ask yourself, 'In order to achieve this, what do we need to

- Start doing

- Stop doing

- Continue doing?'

5. **Jot down what comes to mind.**

Step 3: Checking your gut instinct and intuition.

1. **Refocus your attention as in Step 2.**

2. **Open your eyes again and check what you've jotted down.** Imagine what's on the paper becoming a reality and hold that thought for a moment.

3. **Close your eyes or hold them in soft focus.** Take five slow breaths. Now focus your attention on your body.

- How does your body feel in this moment in time? If you feel any tensions or sensations, where in your body are they being held?

- Do you feel any emotions? What are they?

- Are any thoughts popping into your head? What are they?

4. **Examine your experiences during this exercise.** If you felt excitement and happiness and your body felt fine, you've probably got it right. If you felt fear or uncertainty, you may need to revisit your strategy.

This activity works well with a group. You can lead the mindfulness exercises and segue into and out of planning activities.

Developing strategies mindfully

Having defined a high-level vision, it's time to develop a strategy to make it happen. You need to gather key information into one place and summarise it into an easy-to-read format.

You can use the model shown in Figure 10-1 as a discussion tool.

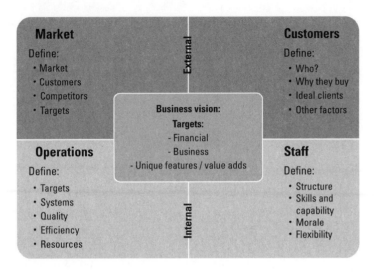

Figure 10-1: Strategy development tool.

Consider conducting a SWOT analysis for each of the segments in the model from Figure 10-1, whereby you identify each segment's:

✔ Strengths

✔ Weaknesses

✔ Opportunities

✔ Threats

You can take a mindful approach to this task as follows:

Stage 1: Getting ready.

1. **Decide on the best people to get the task done and invite them to a meeting.** Identify the mix of skills necessary to create an effective team.

2. **Send a copy of Figure 10-1 (or your own version thereof) to each participant prior to the meeting.** Ask them to come to the meeting with data for their own area relating to each segment.

3. **Create the right environment to enable participants to think outside of the box and innovate.** Ensure that hot and cold drinks, slow-energy-release snacks, such as

oat-based cereal bars, and fruit are available, even if you have to buy them yourself.

Stage 2: Mindfully preparing for productivity.

1. **Ask everyone at the beginning of the meeting to switch off (and not just silence) all mobile devices so that everyone's complete attention stays on the task.**

2. **Ask everyone to capture any concerns they may have on slips of paper and place these in a filing tray placed near the door.**

3. **Invite everyone to take part in a 'centring' exercise.** You may wish to explain to participants some of the science behind mindfulness exercises and why doing them is a good use of their time. Model mindfulness by leading the centring exercise as follows:

   • Invite participants to close their eyes or hold them in soft focus.

   • Invite them to focus their attention on the thoughts that enter their heads, to acknowledge them as 'mental processes' and to let them go without starting to think about them or interacting with them in any way. Tell them that if their minds wander it's fine and when they notice this wandering happening to just gently escort their attention back to the present moment. Allow three minutes for this activity.

   • Invite them to focus on the sensation of breathing, experiencing it as though for the first time. Allow two minutes for this activity.

   • Invite them to focus their attention on any sounds they may be hearing — inside the room, outside the room or even outside the building. Explain that the object of the exercise is to simply observe, not judge or react to the sounds. Allow one minute for this activity.

   • Invite them to open their eyes, ready to work on creating a new strategy.

   Ask those participants who do not wish to try the mindfulness exercise to just sit quietly and observe it.

4. **Recap the overall vision that you're all striving to make reality.** This vision should already have been agreed upon in previous meetings.

Stage 3: Mindfully establishing the status quo.

1. **Appoint five chairpersons — one to focus on each of the five segments.** Split the remaining participants evenly between the five groups.

2. **Explain that everyone will have the opportunity to contribute to all five segments.**

3. **Sound a bell to start the information-sharing and capturing process.** After 15 minutes, sound the bell again and ask each group of participants to move to a new chairperson. Repeat until everyone has had the opportunity to visit all five groups.

4. **Lead another short mindfulness exercise.** Use the three-step focus break from Chapter 4.

Stage 4: Mindfully creating a new strategy.

1. **Share the information gathered.** Make sure that you, and the group as a whole, do not start to judge or categorise — just listen and absorb.

2. **Define as a group the strategies needed to achieve the business vision and targets.** Work your way round the segments one at a time.

3. **Thank the group for all their hard work.** Take responsibility for taking away the draft strategy and producing a professional document for sharing and further discussion.

Embedding new values and behaviours

Now that you have a clear idea of your organisation's culture and vision and a clear strategy for the future, you need to make the plan a reality. The vision and strategy may call for staff to embrace new values, and almost certainly to adopt new behaviours.

Be mindful that old ways of working and behaving are likely to be deeply embedded, especially if they worked well in the past and people have enjoyed and been rewarded (by pay, recognition or a sense of achievement) for working in this way. Don't expect staff to embrace your proposed changes with the same enthusiasm as you. For one thing, you have a head start.

You've already started to rewire the way your brain thinks about working. As you've worked on creating the strategy, your brain has been busily storing new information and making new connections. You're aware of all the factors that led you to create the new strategy, but your team are not.

When you're driving change you're likely to embrace it more quickly, even if you're not wildly enthusiastic about what it involves. Asking people to do things differently can generate all sorts of mental conflicts for them — many of which they may be completely unaware of. If accepted, new ways of doing things are eventually stored by the brain as habits, and these habits in time become more dominant than the work habit circuitry that they're currently using. The process of habit formation can be really slow. The more opportunities that you can create to explore and practise new ways of working, the stronger the brain's neural pathways (circuitry) become.

For some people, the perceived threat of the new way of working may prove too great and they default to old ways of thinking and behaving. Be mindful that they may not be defaulting on purpose as an act of anarchy; they may be largely unaware of how their thoughts, emotions and habits are driving their behaviour.

Mindfulness can be invaluable when you're trying to embed new values and behaviours. It helps you to develop awareness of your hidden mental world. It helps you develop the skill to observe your thoughts, emotions and bodily responses. By developing this awareness, you're able to choose a wise response. As a leader, being able to respond to people and situations mindfully helps you manage yourself better when driving through difficult changes. Mindfulness can help you manage your wellbeing and deal with any personal difficulties or inner conflicts that arise. In addition, you'll be better able to observe when your team members are struggling and can then help them work better with their mind.

In times of change and uncertainty, be kind to yourself and your colleagues. As Chapter 4 describes, self-kindness can help you switch off your fight-or-flight response, making it easier to see things clearly and concentrate.

Remember that how you feel about things is likely to have an impact on your behaviour to others. Your behaviour is likely to have an impact on how others feel, which has an impact on how they behave. By acting as a mindful role model, you make things easier for those around you, and you're likely to feel better too.

If you offer mindfulness training to your staff, it probably won't make an unwelcome change any more palatable. What it can do is help them to become more aware of what's going on in their mental landscape. This awareness gives them the opportunity to bring to the surface thoughts and behaviours that are making them unhappy, stressed or fearful. Knowledge of what's going on in their minds allows them to take control of the situation. They can decide what to do next and focus their energy accordingly.

Creating a More Mindful Organisation

Introducing mindfulness into your organisation can lead to many benefits. Not only is mindfulness likely to improve employees' wellbeing, it may also make them more productive and creative. But does such a thing as a 'mindful organisation' actually exist?

In the 1990s, the concept of the 'learning organisation' was popular. The idea was that an organisation would facilitate information sharing and learning for all members of staff and in this way continuously transform itself. Knowledge management systems were put in place to capture information and share it, and knowledge managers appointed to oversee the whole thing. The problem was that no one really knew what a 'learning organisation' looked like, so it was virtually impossible for organisations to know when they had metamorphosed into this mythical beast. While the idea was good, it became a never-ending journey — rather like that experienced by the crew in *Star Trek* — boldly going where no organisation had gone before ... with no clear final destination.

The idea of becoming 'a mindful organisation' may fall into the same trap. You will probably find it easier and more meaningful to focus on incubating pockets of mindfulness within your organisation. Create spaces for staff to go and spend a few minutes in silence to refocus their efforts, and give staff permission to go to this place for short periods when they need to. Let mindfulness evolve within your organisation, and leave the future to sort itself out. Who knows? In a few years' time many aspects of your organisation may be transformed by mindfulness, but it's best to start with the present moment.

Looking beyond the bottom line is good for the bottom line

Research evidence suggests that mindfulness is likely to be good for your bottom line. Here are a few facts to consider:

- ✔ **Stress is now the top cause of workplace sickness and absence in many countries.** Lost productivity costs money. Studies conducted over the past 40 years conclude that mindfulness is highly effective in reducing stress.

- ✔ **Many workers are now so busy that they're in a constant state of fight or flight.** Practising mindfulness can switch off the brain's fight-or-flight response, improving both wellbeing and the ability to be productive.

- ✔ **A lack of focus and concentration can undermine work performance.** Research shows that mindfulness can improve focus and concentration.

- ✔ **The ability to gain perspective and 'see the bigger picture' is important — especially in times of change.** In recent years, seven independent studies have shown that mindfulness can help you see the bigger picture and set aside personal agendas.

- ✔ **Research into mindfulness and decision-making demonstrates that mindfulness can help you make more rational decisions, not be 'blinded' by past experiences, and come up with more creative solutions.**

- ✔ **Mindfulness has proven effective in helping people manage their emotions better, develop a more positive outlook and prevent burnout.**

The return on investment (ROI) of mindfulness

Little research evidence suggests that spending on personal effectiveness courses or many of the generic 'interpersonal' skills training actually has any impact on a company's bottom line. In contrast, a significant volume of research demonstrates that mindfulness does improve a wide range of desirable work skills such as relationships with colleagues and customers, focus and concentration, strategic thinking, decision-making, and overall resilience. It can also increase staff engagement and productivity.

Setting the sums aside (although the bottom line is important) sometimes by looking beyond it and caring for your employees' wellbeing and making the workplace a great place to be, you gain greater commitment and buy-in from your staff. Measuring the value of staff commitment and wellbeing is clearly impossible, but it can't fail to produce a positive impact all round.

Mindfully improving employee engagement and retention

'Engaged employees' are fully involved in and enthusiastic about their work. This engagement motivates them to work in harmony with their organisation. An employee's positive or negative emotional attachment to their job, colleagues and the organisation as a whole is important. Employee engagement is distinctively different from employee satisfaction, motivation and organisational culture.

Mindfulness can improve employee engagement and retention. Practising mindfulness leads to improved work engagement because it elicits positive emotions and improves psychological functioning.

Mindfully engaging staff

If your company runs an annual staff survey that includes questions relating to employee engagement, you could use these questions as a baseline. Try running a mindfulness pilot (refer to Chapter 8) with the full support of the senior management team and line managers, and compare current responses to those of previous years. You may be surprised at the positivity expressed by staff who have completed the mindfulness course compared with the attitudes of colleagues who didn't attend.

Creating the right work-life balance for all employees

As this book repeatedly stresses, working long hours doesn't increase your productivity, it usually decreases it. The same is true for staff members. Some organisations develop a working culture in which long hours are the norm. Employees feel that they need to be seen to be in the office for more hours than they're paid in order to fit in. Emails are often sent late at night, making other employees feel that they're in some way deficient because they're not working at that hour. In a similar way, some organisations expect staff to be in instant contact outside normal working hours.

As a leader, you have the power to support working practices that promote a healthy balance between people's personal and working lives.

Mindfully balancing life and work

Constant connectivity is bad for performance. Try introducing 'no contact times' and encourage staff to switch off their mobile devices when away from work. Keep an eye on the times that you and other senior managers send emails. If the working style that best suits you involves rest and relaxation after normal working hours and then a little time working in peace late in the evening or first thing in the morning, set your emails to send in normal working hours (you can easily set this system up). By doing so, you're not sending the message to others that they too have to be working late at night or early in the morning.

As Chapter 11 covers, lack of control over workload or working methods can be a major source of stress. Where possible, encourage workers to work in a manner that suits them. Encourage individuality, as long as core work hours are covered, work gets done and targets are met.

Offer staff mindfulness training to examine objectively their current work-life balance and to establish a way of working that is more nourishing and rewarding for them personally.

Offer staff a 'quiet room' to go to when they need 10 minutes of silence to regain their sense of balance and improve their productivity. Doing so sends a positive message to staff that their need for a few minutes of quiet mindfulness is recognised; providing this area is so much better than employees sneaking off to store cupboards or toilet cubicles.

Mindfulness can transform both your own and your employees' perception of change and how to manage it. Fortunately, your organisation can become more mindful while still keeping a keen eye on the bottom line. Introducing mindful work practices into your organisation can be difficult when you occupy a junior role, but as a leader you can use your power and influence to change things for the better. You can choose to continue leading as you always have, or start to model some mindful behaviour and start a quiet revolution. You have the power — the choice is yours.

Chapter 11

Ten Ways to Mindfully Manage Work Pressures

*H*owever good you are at your job or happy you are in your work, at some time or other you'll feel under pressure. This chapter looks at some of the most commonly experienced pressures and some ways that mindfulness can help you deal with them.

The UK Health and Safety Executive (HSE) identified six factors that can lead to work-related stress if they're not managed properly: Demands, control, support, relationships, role and change. This chapter starts by exploring these six factors before moving on to some more general pressures you may encounter at some time or another.

Mindfully Coping with Inappropriate Work Demands

In the current economic climate, many organisations are looking at ways to cut costs. Making people redundant is often an obvious solution. Unfortunately for those left behind, fewer staff means greater workloads and increased responsibilities. While some people may thrive in this situation, seeing it as a way to acquire new experience and improve their prospects for promotion, others may struggle to meet the new demands of their jobs.

At the other end of the spectrum, some job roles are being de-skilled. This situation too can be a source of pressure as work becomes less stimulating and meaningful, and fewer opportunities for promotion exist.

When you're next feeling overwhelmed by your workload, step away from it for a short while. Spend a few minutes practising mindfulness to help put things back in perspective. Doing so will save you time in the long run because you'll return to the task at hand feeling more focused as your stress level declines.

Spend ten or more minutes practising your favourite mindfulness exercise. Try mindfulness of breath, a body scan or using thoughts or sounds as the focus for your attention. Immediately afterwards, choose something to work on that gives you a sense of personal satisfaction or a feeling of control over your work.

If doing a spot of mindfulness isn't possible, try giving your full attention to just one task and aim to get it finished. If you catch your mind wandering on to other things you need to do, kindly and gently escort your attention back to the task you're working on. When you've finished the task, acknowledge its completion and congratulate yourself on a job well done. Now you can go on to your next job.

Mindfully Dealing with a Lack of Control over Your Work

Feeling a lack of control over your work can rapidly lead to stress and poor performance. This situation is true whatever your job role — from senior executive to manual worker. Workplace health and safety organisations all over the world agree that having no power to decide on how a job is done is a major cause of workplace stress and frequently makes employees, at all levels in the organisation, unwell.

Try this exercise when your thoughts are whirling or you're feeling angry or frustrated:

1. **Spend a minute observing your emotions.** What are they? What impact (if any) are they having on your body? Are you holding any tension? If so, where? Are your emotions triggering any thoughts? Try to just observe what's happing in this present moment; don't try to start fixing things.

2. **Spend a minute observing your thoughts.** Remember to observe them with openness and curiosity. You don't need to change them or make them go away. Just observe them as they come and go.

3. **Spend a minute focusing on the present-moment sensation of breathing.** Feel the breath coming in and the breath going out.

4. **Ask yourself what, in this present moment, you do have control over.** Write these things down or record them on your smartphone.

Mindfully Managing a Lack of, or Inappropriate, Support

If you're offered a promotion, you'll probably be very pleased won't you? But a promotion can turn into nightmare if you receive inadequate support from colleagues, peers and senior staff. This situation is true for all staff, from the most senior to the most junior.

Get mindful. Identify the help you really need at this moment in time. If you can't see the wood for the trees, stop what you're doing and practise some mindfulness. Don't worry about the bigger picture — you can fix that later. Ask for the guidance or support you need. Don't waste energy worrying about what people might think; doing so usually causes more suffering and wastes more time than actually asking the question! If you still don't get the clear guidance you need, ask in writing via a letter or email. Be polite and concise — keep it short to read and short to answer.

Mindfully Managing Difficult Working Relationships

Whatever your job role, a big part of working life is interacting with your colleagues. For many people, this chance to socialise can be a source of enjoyment, learning and fulfilment. It can transform a dull, low-paid job into something that makes you feel good about yourself and to which you look forward to every day.

On the flip side, some people are subjected to unacceptable behaviour from colleagues ranging from bullying to discrimination in all its forms. If you were treated badly outside work, you'd probably walk away. You'd probably also take appropriate action to stop people from making you unhappy. Unfortunately, things aren't so simple at work.

Try a befriending exercise such as 'Cultivating kindness' (refer to Chapter 4). It may help you see things in a different way or reduce the level of tension induced by the people you find difficult.

If things don't get easier, practising mindfulness regularly will help ease tension and emotional reactivity. It may also help you stand back and gain a greater perspective. If fixing things or finding a different way to relate to the difficult person are impossible, take steps to regain control over the situation. Speak in confidence to someone in the human resources department. Talk to your boss, or even your boss's boss. If things can't be made better, start looking for a new job and, for your remaining time in the company, keep reminding yourself that this problem isn't forever, it will pass. Life's too short to remain unhappy.

Mindfully Gaining Clarity about Your Job Role

In most roles, you're judged based on your ability to do your job to the required standard. But what if you have no job description? What if you don't understand what your job description really means in terms of expected outcomes? What if your job description doesn't match the job you're being asked to do? What if the rules keep changing but nobody tells you?

These scenarios are all too common. We know of many people who have no job description, despite having asked for one. This situation can lead to them missing out work that their managers deem important (despite not telling them so!), or working hard on things that the organisation doesn't value. We know of other employees who do have clearly defined job descriptions but they're not updated in line with organisational changes.

If you find yourself in any of these situations, decide for yourself what your work priorities should be and tactfully let your boss know. If you're unsure, try practising mindfulness. Doing so may help you gain perspective and decide what you really need in the present moment.

Mindfully Navigating the Bumpy Road of Frequent Change

As Chapter 4 discusses, many employees are now subjected to constant, ongoing change. While change may now be the norm, humans dislike uncertainty, and change creates uncertainty. When you're faced with an uncertain future, your threat system almost certainly kicks in, putting your primitive brain in control (refer to Chapter 1).

Mindfulness can help you reduce your sense of being under threat, and put your higher brain back in control. Use mindfulness of breath on a regular basis (refer to Chapter 3). When your mind wanders and you start thinking, observe the thoughts that arise in a detached manner. After your mindfulness practice, reflect on any patterns or common themes that emerged. Try to bring some conscious attention to what specific thoughts are unsettling you. Reflect on how much of the discomfort or suffering you're experiencing is self-induced — self-generated by your attempts to predict the future. Make a wise decision on what to do next.

Changing the way you work (even when you really want to!) is often a slow process. Mindfulness can help you to bring conscious awareness to what you're thinking and feeling, and to recognise how your thoughts and feelings impact on your behaviour. With a little regular mindfulness practice, you'll be able to more quickly identify when you're falling into old patterns of thoughts and behaviours, and consciously decide on a skilful course of action.

Mindfully Dealing with Difficult One-to-One Meetings

Other people can be the most challenging aspect of your working day. You might be faced with a colleague who agrees with a plan of action, then goes off and does her own thing. You may experience conflict with a peer over a difference of opinion; this situation can turn ugly and be harmful to working relationships. Maybe you're one of those people who try to avoid conflict whenever possible? Conflict avoidance is very common in workplaces. Unfortunately, steering clear of disagreement and conflict or leaving things unsaid often results in anxiety and further tension.

Mindfulness can be really valuable when dealing with conflict in one-to-one meetings. Bear these tips in mind:

- ✔ **Try to resist the urge to judge or make assumptions.** Step back, freeing yourself from past baggage and stepping into the present moment with an open mind. Deal with any issues that arise if and when they actually do so.

- ✔ **Manage your emotional response to the situation.** Anger and frustration are very human responses when you're experiencing difficulty with others. Unfortunately, they're unlikely to help and may make things a whole lot worse. While you can't manage the emotional responses of other people — you can manage your own. Practising mindfulness makes you more consciously aware of your own emotional state, and thus better able to regulate and manage it.

- ✔ **Tuning in to the present moment.** You'll be able to respond more skilfully to the situation instead of reacting based on old mental programming that may be inappropriate.

Mindfully Coping with the Threat of Redundancy

Threat of redundancy can be a very worrying time. While you may not have any control over whether you're made redundant or not, you do have control over how much you suffer.

Naturally, being under threat of redundancy is a cause of anxiety, but if you step back and think about it, losing sleep at night and worrying yourself sick won't actually help matters. First and foremost, be kind to yourself. It's okay to feel worried or frightened — acknowledge that that's how you feel, and then get on with something else.

Take time out to linger on and appreciate the good things in your life. They may be as simple as a car with a tank of fuel that safely and comfortably gets you from A to B. It may be coffee with a good friend or a hug from your child. Really pause to soak up the good from these moments.

When you do realise that you're spiralling into negative thoughts, don't get angry with yourself — it only adds fuel to the fire. Just acknowledge that you're starting to spiral, bring yourself back to the present moment, and get on with what you need to do.

Mindfully Coping with Redundancy Survivor Syndrome

If you're 'lucky' enough to survive a round of redundancies, you may fall victim to redundancy survivor syndrome.

Redundancies make things uncomfortable for all employees. Many employers make great efforts to support and care for staff facing redundancy. Few plan for the survivors who keep their jobs — assuming that they're just pleased and relieved to still have a job. Employees who survive redundancy may experience initial relief, but this relief can quickly turn into guilt because they've kept their jobs while others have been forced to leave. They can even feel envious of their colleagues' redundancy payments and their chance to embark on a new life. A few months down the line, the survivors may ultimately feel resentful about the extra work they have to do to cover the work of those who have left.

As in the previous section, just remember to be kind to yourself. Experiencing these sorts of feelings is completely natural (even if they're unhelpful at times). Accepting your feelings without trying to change them often reduces their grip on you and can provide welcome relief.

Using Mindfulness to Reduce Stress

Some stress is necessary — this stress is what makes you get out of bed in the morning and motivates you to do your best. However, excessive stress is bad both for the individual and in terms of a firm's productivity. Work-related stress is a widespread problem, and isn't confined to specific sectors or job roles. Stress can affect anyone at any time in any business. Stress is also a major cause of sickness absence and staff turnover. If you're very stressed, you may make errors at work and your inability to focus may mean that you waste lots of time.

Mindfulness is proven to reduce stress. A little mindfulness practised daily can reduce your tendency to feel stressed out or depressed. It can also enable you to recognise when you're starting to feel excessively stressed, and to take steps to get things back in balance. Spotting the symptoms of stress early enables you to take the mindful steps necessary to regain equilibrium. As little as three minutes of mindfulness may be all it takes. If you ignore the early warning signs, it may take you much longer to return to peak performance — you might have to take time off work or even use medication. Suffering from stress at times is inevitable, how long you suffer for is up to you. Mindfulness puts this choice in your hands.

Index

About the Authors

Shamash Alidina, MEng MA PGCE, is CEO of Learn Mindfulness International, offering training and teacher training in mindfulness for the general public, as well as for life and executive coaches, yoga teachers, doctors, nurses and other health professionals. His website offers online mindfulness courses and online mindfulness teacher training. He continues to grow his offer of audio CDs, books and more.

Shamash offers mindfulness workshops several times a year around the world and a limited number of one-to-one mindfulness coaching sessions in person in London, or via phone/Skype.

Shamash has trained extensively in mindfulness at Bangor University's Centre for Mindfulness in the UK, and with Dr Jon Kabat-Zinn and Dr Saki Santorelli in New York. He holds a Masters Degree in Engineering (Imperial College) and a Masters Degree in Education (Open University), with a focus on Brain and Behaviour.

Shamash has appeared on television, radio, and in magazines and newspapers including on the BBC and in the *Daily Express*. He hosts a mindfulness radio show at www.mindfulnessradio.com, which has had several thousand listeners. He is an international speaker, addressing audiences at places like Cambridge University's conference on Mindfulness in the Workplace, the Mind and its Potential conference in Sydney, and the Healthy Living Show in Auckland.

Shamash is the author of the international bestsellers *Mindfulness For Dummies* and *Relaxation For Dummies* (both Wiley).

See all of Shamash's courses and workshops at www.learnmindfulness.co.uk or email him directly at shamash@learnmindfulness.co.uk.

Catch Shamash on the social networks at: www.twitter.com/shamashalidina, www.facebook.com/learnmindfulness and www.linkedin.com/in/learnmindfulness.

Juliet Adams MSc, FCIPD, is Director of A Head for Work, specialising in management development and new approaches to leadership. She develops bespoke learning programmes and e-learning content for leading organisations around the world. She designs and delivers mindfulness at work courses based on MBCT, but specially adapted to meet the demands and expectations of the workplace. She teaches mindfulness to groups of staff in the workplace and offers one-to-one mindfulness coaching for senior staff in person across the UK. Where face-to-face working is impractical, Juliet works with clients online via live interactive web meeting technology.

Juliet has spent most of her career working with organisations on leadership and strategic learning programmes, organisational development, and change projects. She has worked on national projects for the police and several standards-setting bodies. She also advises and supports senior HR staff to help them make their HR or L&D function more strategic and business focussed. She holds a Masters Degree in Training and Performance Management and is a Fellow of CIPD.

In recent years Juliet has become increasingly involved in bringing mindfulness to the world of work. She is the founder of Mindfulnet.org, a leading web-based independent mindfulness information resource. She arranged the first Mindfulness at Work conference at Robinson College Cambridge in 2012, and the second with Cranfield University's School of Management.

Juliet has been interviewed by the *Daily Telegraph*, BBC and *Personnel Today* and is a regular commentator on mindfulness at work. She lives in Cambridgeshire near the beautiful city of Ely.

See Juliet's courses and workshops at www.aheadforwork.co.uk or email her directly at juliet@aheadforwork.co.uk. Catch Juliet on the social networks at: www.twitter.com/mindfulnet or www.twitter.com/A_Head_for_Work and www.linkedin.com/in/julietadams.

Publisher's Acknowledgements

We're proud of this book; please send us your comments through our online registration form located at dummies.custhelp.com.

Some of the people who helped bring this book to market include the following:

Acquisitions, Editorial and Media Development

Editorial Manager: Dani Karvess

Acquisitions Editor: Kerry Laundon

Production

Graphics: diacriTech

Proofreader: Kerry Laundon

Indexer: Don Jordan, Antipodes Indexing

The authors and publisher would like to thank the following copyright holders, organisations and individuals for their permission to reproduce copyright material in this book:

- **Cover Image:** © iStock.com/filmfoto

Every effort has been made to trace the ownership of copyright material. Information that enables the publisher to rectify any error or omission in subsequent editions is welcome. In such cases, please contact the Legal Services section of John Wiley & Sons Australia, Ltd.

Business & Investing

978-1-118-22280-5
$39.95

978-0-73031-945-0
$19.95

978-0-73031-951-1
$19.95

978-0-73031-065-5
$19.95

978-0-73030-584-2
$24.95

978-1-11864-126-2
$19.95

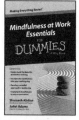

978-0-73031-949-8
$19.95

978-0-73031-954-2
$19.95

978-0-730-31069-3
$39.95

978-1-118-57255-9
$34.95

978-1-742-16998-9
$45.00

978-1-118-64122-4
$39.95

Order today! Contact your Wiley sales representative.

Available in print and e-book formats.